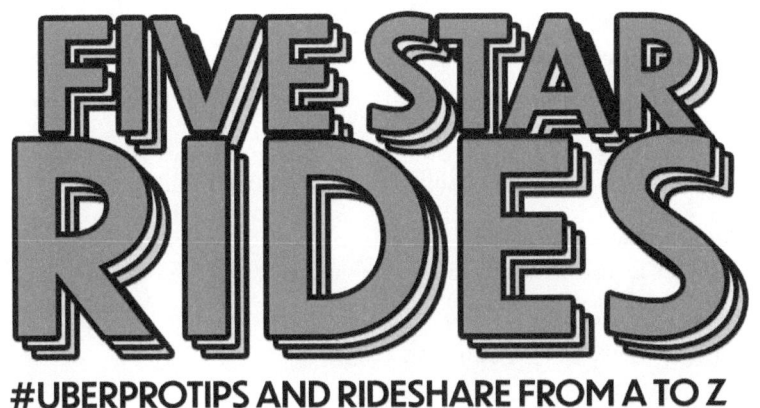

FIVE STAR RIDES

#UBERPROTIPS AND RIDESHARE FROM A TO Z

NATE LIVESAY

Published by Argyle Fox Publishing | argylefoxpublishing.com

Publisher holds no responsibility for content of this work. Content is the sole responsibility of the author.

ISBN 979-8-89124-021-6 (Paperback)
ISBN 979-8-89124-020-9 (Hardcover)
ISBN 979-8-89124-022-3 (Ebook)

ARGYLE FOX
PUBLISHING

To the unheard and the unseen,
To the dismissive and condescending,
To the generous and the grateful,
To the drunk and disorderly—
Without all of you, this book never makes it to print.

TABLE OF CONTENTS

INTRODUCTION

You want a way to make some extra money and decide to check out this new app called Uber. It seems simple enough. You try it out in your small town, giving a handful of rides to unremarkable passengers. Now, you're hungry to make some real money. So, you decide on a late shift in Hilton Head Island, South Carolina, during the heat of tourist season.

You start driving a little after 9 p.m. The app pings, you drive to the location, find your passenger, deposit them at their destination, and then find out how much you've earned. Three hours in, you've already banked $70.

Some rides are easy—the passengers wait outside for you and are nearly sober. It's easy to get in and out of the restaurant and hotel parking lots. Some rides are more complicated. The passengers aren't ready when you arrive, or they aren't where said they would be. Or they're not sober enough to identify which villa they're staying in for the week.

The fares rise as it gets later, matching the degree of difficulty for pickups and drop-offs. Some mental calculations convince you that if things go well, you can make another $100 tonight and still get home just after 3 a.m.

The app pings and you get back to work, picturing that crisp Benjamin in your account.

FIVE STAR RIDES

Your next pickup is at a bar in The BarMuda Triangle, the busiest night spot on the island. You get there, and your passenger isn't ready to go. She ignores your messages and calls. After five minutes of waiting, you cancel the ride.

Soon enough, you find out this is a regular occurrence at late night spots. People change their mind, find another ride, pass out. Whatever the reason, rides often don't work out.

Fortunately for you, as soon as you cancel that ride, another takes its place. Better yet, the passenger is at the same location. To top it off, this is a surge ride—a big surge, a 4.5. In rideshare language, this means you'll make four and a half times the normal fare.

Excited, you arrive at the pin, greeted by a mass of people. Less exciting, none of them are looking for you. Eventually, a very drunk dude staggers to your car and asks if you're his driver. Since you're there to pick up Lindsay, you happily explain that you aren't his driver.

A few minutes pass. You call Lindsay. No answer. The wait-time timer (how long you're required to wait for delinquent passengers) has reached zero, so you can cancel the ride. But it's a risk. Cancel the ride, and you make $3.75 instead of the $25-plus if you get Lindsay home.

You call Lindsay again. A very drunk lady answers, asking where you are. Communication is difficult, but you see her in the distance. Somehow, you get past all the drinks she's had recently and reach her brain, explaining that if she turns around, she'll see your car. She succeeds and leads her equally drunk friends toward your Civic.

Unfortunately, the story doesn't end with a happy ending. Nothing is ever that simple.

Just as Lindsay reaches your car, she doubles over and vomits by your front bumper. Lindsay's friends ask you to wait a few more minutes while they get her cleaned up so she can go home. You've already waited for ten minutes, and you get pennies until the ride starts. Time for a decision: keep waiting because it's a surge ride or cut your losses and head to the next ride?

Lindsay may have splashed vomit on your front bumper, but her friends were nice. You agree to wait a couple more minutes. They reemerge with a cleaned-up Lindsay, and all four ladies cram into the car.

You start the ride and are thrilled to learn you have definitely made the right decision. The ride is taking you back to Beaufort, where you live. Doesn't happen often, but you'll make at least $100 on this ride, and it's putting you at your doorstep before 3 a.m., just as planned.

All goes well. Lindsay keeps her stomach contents in her stomach and leaves your car smelling relatively decent. You even snuggle into your bed before two a.m., $200 richer. This isn't a bad gig, you tell yourself as you drift off the sleep.

That night, driving strangers around in your car wasn't a bad gig. But most nights don't go like that. You have no idea what lies ahead of you over the next 10,000 rides.

I can't explain my disbelief that I've given more than 10,000 rides through Uber and Lyft. Ten years ago, I would have laughed at the idea that I would give a single ride. In fact, the first time I mentioned the idea to my wife, that's exactly what she did. Looking back, I can see it was a crazy idea, but the world brings some crazy twists. Much like an Uber ride, you never know where life will take you.

FIVE STAR RIDES

I spent years of my working life as a public-school teacher and basketball coach. Somehow, I managed to transition into another service job that paid even less, serving as Director of Economic Empowerment at World Orphans. There, I developed and oversaw a microloan program for the small, international nonprofit. While our work in Haiti, Guatemala, Uganda, and Ethiopia was fulfilling and meaningful, it left a void in my bank account that made it difficult to afford a mortgage, two cars, a wife, three kids, and a dog. I needed more cash.

I was willing to work for it, but there was a catch. My second job had to be flexible. My job required regular international travel, and the aforementioned kids and wife demanded my time and attention as well. Enter the rideshare side hustle. As a rideshare driver, I could drive on my own schedule. By giving up a little sleep and some free time, I could easily carve out twenty or thirty hours of late-night and weekend drive time.

Signing up and getting started was easy. In exchange for my personal information, Uber and Lyft ran background checks and investigated my driving record. Forty-eight hours later I was cleared to drive. The only remaining step was to take my Honda Civic to a mechanic for a vehicle inspection. The inspection took less than thirty minutes and cost $25.

Less than a week after my initial inspiration, I was ready to hit the road.

Like everything else, rideshare driving has a significant learning curve. I made a lot of mistakes early on. Each one taught me a little more about pickups, drop-offs, and passenger preferences. Just when I thought I had it figured out, I would encounter a new situation and have to rethink my entire strategy.

I had to figure out how the app worked, then I had to learn my way around the low country of South Carolina and Coastal Georgia. Rides took me as far north as Columbia, South Carolina, and as far south as Brunswick, Georgia. Each location provided unique obstacles and experiences that required different tactics and strategies to make driving worth the time and effort.

I figured out quickly that I could make decent money as long as I was smart. That meant having a winning strategy for when and where I drove and what rides I accepted. Though tempting to accept every trip in hopes of maximizing earnings, this only leads to nights of driving all over without making much money.

Even with a great plan, a night's success largely came down to luck of the draw. I never knew with certainty where rides were going or what I would make on a ride until it ended. That said, I maximized my chances of success by paying attention so I could make educated guesses about which rides were most likely to pay best.

Equally disheartening was that car expenses piled up quickly, and the amount of money the app promised was rather optimistic. Unstable wages weren't the only new part. While I had spent two decades in service-oriented jobs, I never dealt with random strangers at varying levels of sobriety. After just a few weekends of late-night weekend driving, it was evident that I would learn a lot about human nature while shuttling people from place to place.

By nature, I'm analytical, realistic, and somewhat cynical.

Despite this, I was still shocked at how clueless or awful people can be. They're impatient, rude, condescending, and nasty. And somehow, even when they're incoherent, they remain demanding.

Sometimes, their attitudes made me mad. At other times, they made me sad. On good nights, crazy customers made me shake my head and laugh.

Ever been called a motherfu**er because you wouldn't take someone to Taco Bell? I have.

Ever received a sincere thank you and $20 tip because you stopped the car to let a dad buy ice cream for his kids on the way home? I have.

I saw and heard things I'd never seen or heard. My passengers gave me a window into humanity that I never experienced before. Suppose it's the mixture of alcohol and anonymity—a very revealing combination.

Obviously, every rider wasn't a nightmare. Some were hilarious. Some were fun. Some were genuinely interesting. Most I don't even remember. Generally, passengers just wanted to reach their destination and were thrilled that their phones could summon someone to pick them up quickly and inexpensively. Because I'm in the South, there were lots of conversations about the weather and SEC football. But some people were more than I could have imagined. These select few were walking embodiments of the SMH emoji.

I didn't just learn about people. I also learned how technology companies work—how they gather our data and use artificial intelligence (AI) to make their products and business models function. They package improvements and updates as "making the world a better place," but all

FIVE-STAR
RIDES

ARTIFICIAL INTELLIGENCE & ALGORITHMS

"There are lies, damn lies, and statistics."

—Mark Twain

#UberProTip—Keep your phone charged at the end of the night. It is possible that your ride home will cost you more if your battery is about to die.

You are being manipulated. Don't feel bad, you aren't alone. We're all being manipulated. From governments to coffee shops, persuading you to think what they want you to think is big business. Millions of dollars get spent on it every day.

The most effective tactics are those we don't realize are being used on us. With a job well done, they can convince us that they're trying to improve our lives, not just their bottom line.

Because this is big business, many corporations turn

19

to technology—specifically customized algorithms and specialized AI—to mine the data we give them so they can effectively target us.

When I decided to drive for Uber, I didn't realize how much my life would be affected by AI and algorithms. When I chose to give rideshare driving a try, the concept hadn't yet gained mass understanding. This was before Uber became ubiquitous, when it was considered a new, improved, innocent substitute for taxis and rental cars.

At the time, Uber was practically unknown in my small, coastal South Carolina town. Every night I took people on their first Uber ride. When I told friends I was moonlighting as an Uber driver, half asked what Uber was. Remember those days?

In addition to being an income source, rideshare driving provided a ride-by-ride master's degree in human behavior. Want to learn about people? Drive someone you don't know. Want to learn even more? Drive that same person when he's drunk.

I've never been a bartender, but I've driven a lot of them. Seems to me that being an rideshare driver is similar, as you interact with the best and worst of humanity. Because of the anonymous nature of the interaction, you see people real and raw. They don't know you, they won't ever see you again, and they don't have any facades to maintain.

Some of them want to talk, and some don't know when to shut up. Some passengers invite you into their joy, while others unleash their pain on you. Keep your eyes and ears open, and you'll learn from each passenger, and what they tell you is only the tip of the iceberg. Watch how they interact with you and other passengers.

Do they make requests or demands? Are they grateful for your service or treat you like hired help? Does alcohol loosen their inhibitions and bring out a fun-loving, happy personality? Or does alcohol empower their selfish, entitled side? Are they interested in learning about you or do they suspect you're poor and stupid for driving for a rideshare company?

If a rider talks on the phone, you hear one side of her conversation, but it's telling. You hear her word choice and tone. When you go to pick someone up, you see his pickup location and destination. You sense how those locations impact the rider's mood. You see how he looks, dresses, and smells. All those things tell a story as well.

Then you continue learning about your passenger after the ride is over. Does she slam the door or not even bother to close it? Does he tip? Is the tip because of you or because of her? Did she leave something important behind? Did he take their trash or leave the car a mess?

As I drove longer, I realized how many of our interactions are influenced by the rideshare companies and their algorithms. The initial phase of their business model is to ruthlessly eliminate competition with artificially low fares. Finding success in that objective, the company's C-suites shift their focus to maximizing profit by exploiting passengers and drivers. Thanks to this, when you arrive at a pickup, you and your passenger may be in a bad mood because of how the company arranged the meeting. The rider may get charged triple the normal fare. Three previous drivers may have canceled on them. And the algorithm may switch you from a profitable, easy ride to a more difficult, lower-paying gig. Or the app may send you to the wrong location or give you a terrible route to get there.

All these things affect the ride's vibe. Yet it happens every day. The companies gather massive amounts of data from their drivers and passengers, combine it with research on human behavior, plug it into advanced AI, and an algorithm gets birthed that manipulates and exploits all involved parties in order to maximize profit.

Rideshare companies depend on ride volume to make money. Base fares and service fees get added to every ride before time and distance are considered. These fees go straight to the company. On many rides, these fees make up the bulk of the company's profit. Translation: They need as many drivers on the road as possible at all times. To make that happen, the companies need every driver to accept every ride offered to them.

A declined ride on one app might cause a passenger to use another app or a taxi. The disgruntled rider may even give up on a ride and just walk. Any of these options costs Uber and Lyft market share, decreases profits, and lowers their leverage with the entities they negotiate with.

On the other side of the coin, rideshare companies need customers to believe a ride will be nearby every time they open the app. To ensure this, companies use every tool available to persuade, manipulate, or force drivers to accept every ride offered to them. Incentives, threats, and manipulation are the main tools for increasing acceptance rates.

Because Uber and Lyft control information, they have ultimate control, empowering executives to calculate and execute a plan to charge each passenger as much as possible while they pay each driver as little as possible. Fares and bonuses vary by market based on what the algorithm decides is best for the bottom line. No two drivers are treated exactly the same. They are offered different fares for the same ride. They receive different incentives even in the same market. The algorithm incentivizes behaviors they want with rewards and punishes drivers for unwanted behaviors. At the same time, the rideshare companies spend millions annually on lobbying and advertising campaigns, insisting their drivers are independent contractors, not employees.

DESIGN

The driver app is gamified with sounds and lights curated to increase the number of rides drivers accept. Picture the tools casinos use to keep customers on the gaming floor, playing games deep into the night. Rideshare companies use the same mechanics and psychology to manipulate drivers into staying online and accepting rides in hopes of hitting that jackpot ride where they finally beat the house. But just like in Vegas, the rideshare house always wins.

The game begins when the ride offer flashes on the screen with an audio notification. Move fast though, because the notification is around for a limited amount of time before disappearing. There's no time to process and make an informed decision about whether or not to accept the ride. You also don't know when the next offer will appear and whether it'll be a better gig or worse. So, you take a gamble.

After all, declining rides has consequences. Rideshare companies create friction for drivers who decline rides. A pop-up message may appear or you get logged out of the app. These are another tactic reminding drivers that everything runs smoother when you accept every ride offered.

Through sounds, flashes, and artificial uncertainty, rideshare companies use psychology to manipulate drivers into accepting more rides than they otherwise would.

BONUSES & INCENTIVES

Because base pay per ride is so poor, Uber and Lyft use streaks and bonuses to motivate drivers to accept more rides—especially rides not worth taking. These bonuses can significantly impact earnings, so almost all drivers accept any ride to achieve these incentives.

Streaks are tied to the number of consecutive rides you accept. Three consecutive rides in a two-hour window could net a bonus between $9 and $21. Or the bonus may come when you accept three consecutive rides in a certain geographical area within ninety minutes.

These bonuses convince drivers to accept rides during peak demand or to take on passengers in areas with longer wait times and therefore fewer ride opportunities. Often, the bonus is more than what a driver earns in fares. Reach the bonus, and you more than double your earnings.

When rideshare companies are desperate for drivers, they offer crazy bonuses. I've seen them give $100 for completing three rides, but such bonuses are few and far between.

Making bonuses more complicated is the variance. Bonuses change from market to market and even from driver to driver. All is driven by the algorithm, which focuses on maximizing profit. Because of this, rideshare companies can pay drivers different amounts for the same job. The number of drivers typically has an inverse relationship with the economy. As inflation increases and the economy declines, driver numbers increase. As the number of rideshare drivers increases, bonuses decrease in value and frequency.

Other bonuses are volume based. Earn the bonus by completing a certain number of rides in a certain time period. Some are worth a few dollars per ride and worth relentlessly pursuing. Others are so bad they're laughable. For example, you may get a $50 to $150 bonus for completing twenty to sixty rides, Monday through Thursday. Then you may get $100 to $200 for a similar amount of rides during peak weekends in peak locations. The next week, complete fifty rides to earn $30—a bonus of 60 cents per ride.

Although there's no external way to confirm this, many drivers believe the algorithm throttles ride requests when drivers close in on the more profitable bonuses. In other words, the algorithm actively sabotages drivers' ability to make more money. Based on my personal experience, the idea is likely true. Any time I creep up on a profitable bonus, I get notified of considerably fewer rides.

From the perspective of rideshare companies, the ideal driver is desperate, bad at math, and driving a clean, reliable car. High inflation, rising gas prices, and bloated car prices are bad for most people, but they're great for Uber and Lyft. Anything that makes it tougher for people to afford the purchase and maintenance of their vehicles ensures a steady supply of people desperate for another source of income.

With such a frustrating system, rideshare drivers don't last very long. Since the companies need as many drivers as possible, they offer other incentives to keep the driver pipeline full at all times. Need to drive but don't have a car? In many markets, they'll rent one to you by the week. What this accomplishes is threefold:

1. If you don't have a personal vehicle, driving for a rideshare company will allow you to have one—a powerful incentive to drive.

2. Technology in rental cars inform rideshare companies if you go offline due to car problems.

3. Paying weekly rent to the company guarantees you'll drive more. After all, you can't make any money each week until paying the week's car rent.

More drivers taking more rides results in an improved bottom line. With that in mind, the final bonus is a startup bonus. Depending on timing, the economy, and the local market, companies offer new drivers bonuses ranging from $200 to $2,000. New drivers also get bonuses for taking a set amount of rides during their first thirty, sixty, or ninety days. These incentives are a powerful way to keep new drivers on the road and create a psychological mirage as to how much money a driver can make.

THREATS & PUNISHMENTS

If app design and incentives don't work, threats might. For a long time, Lyft and Uber used outright threats to keep acceptance rates high and cancellation rates low. They threatened deactivation if drivers didn't maintain acceptably high acceptance rates and low cancellation rates. They also kept this threat prominent inside the app.

As the blatant threats led to public relations issues and

legal challenges, they sought out ways to "prove" that drivers are independent contractors. One way they did this was to switch from the stick of deactivation to the carrot of driver tier benefits.

To reach the top level and be a platinum driver, drivers must accrue a certain number of points. Additionally, they must maintain an acceptance rate of nearly 100 percent, cancellation rate of nearly zero, and a high driver rating from passengers.

Regular drivers have no problem earning points and keeping a good driver rating. When you need a quick point bump, just take a few less desirable rides. Not willing to take every ride that pops up on your screen? You'll have a hard time maintaining required acceptance and cancellation rates. Despite not making obvious threats, they make it clear that they expect high rates. They do this with the techniques mentioned above. For a while, if you declined consecutive rides, a so-called glitch in the app logged you out of the app. Then, you had to login again before you could accept more rides. That "glitch" has been corrected. Now they just take you offline when you decline or cancel rides more than they think you should.

"GLITCHES"

Because app design, incentives, and threats aren't enough to ensure 100-percent compliance, it appears the companies manipulate or intentionally deceive drivers. Since streak and bonus earnings affect driver behavior, they give drivers false information to decrease the number of rides they decline.

Example: The app sends push notifications to drivers'

phones that they lost eligibility for a bonus streak by not accepting a ride. However, the whole thing is a scam. The drivers were never eligible for that bonus streak in their driving areas.

The app also manipulates time or distance information given to drivers before accepting rides. Time and distance information provided before a ride often doesn't match the actual time or distance of the ride. I only get accurate information after accepting the ride. Interestingly, the time and distance are always longer than initially disclosed.

If you could sit in a corporate meeting at Lyft or Uber, I imagine their nightmare would be for a passenger to not get a ride in a timely fashion. If this happens, the passenger may use another company to complete this trip. If that trip goes well, the passenger may stick with that company for all their future rideshare needs. Uber and Lyft can't allow that to happen. To prevent it, they empty their bag of tricks.

Because the algorithm has an infinite amount of data about rides and riders, IT experts can easily discover trends. One trend is that ride requests in certain locations are less likely to be accepted by drivers—especially where markets aren't oversaturated with desperate drivers. If there's no parking in a certain location, rides will get declined. Too many short trips that don't pay much? More declined rides.

There's no real way to know why drivers don't accept requests, but the algorithm notices the problem. Uber's answer? Glitches that never show up at any other time.

Glitch 1: A ride pops up with no upfront information. All you see is the time from destination and a rider rating. Accept a ride like that in my market, and you inevitably wind up on a military installation or another difficult pickup location after multiple drivers declined the ride (often, you already declined the ride at least once). Even worse, the destination is three or more hours away and you can't possibly make money without spending all day on one trip and negotiating a cash tip ahead of time.

Glitch 2: This one's even more savage. The companies never show you the exact pickup address ahead of time. They provide a general location, the closest intersections. But sometimes, if Uber or Lyft are having a particularly difficult time getting a driver to accept a ride, they show a location one or two blocks away. It may be just enough to hide the actual location, but sometimes the locations are off by miles. Last time this happened to me, I used Google Maps, which showed the actual pickup location was off by nine minutes and more than four miles. The rideshare app used an intersection from the wrong island in an attempt to get me to take a ride I had repeatedly declined.

This is why I don't care about cancellation rates. Any time they attempt to manipulate me into taking nonsensical rides, I message the passenger, explain what happened, and cancel the ride.

I suppose it's possible that these really are innocent glitches. I'm certain the rideshare companies would say so. It's definitely possible that I've experienced years of bad luck and that other glitches make pickups easier and more profitable, but after more than 10,000 rideshare trips, it seems just as likely that this is another example of the algorithm attempting to manipulate driver behavior.

PASSENGERS GET IT, TOO

The algorithm did it.

While they will never admit it, rideshare companies design their algorithm around a simple goal: use all available data to create pricing that maximizes the charge for a ride and keep enough drivers on the road so that one is always willing to pick up passengers quickly for the lowest possible fare, maximizing customer satisfaction and the spread between customer fare and driver pay.

How do they do this? Rideshare companies don't just use psychology to manipulate drivers. They do the same thing with customers.

Believe it or not, the cost of your ride is only partially tied to how long your trip is. It has nothing to do with how much they will pay the driver. In each market they show a rate card that explains the per-mile and per-minute cost of each ride. These rates vary as much as 300 percent from market to market, but they use far more data than this to price your trip.

If they give you an upfront price, they don't have to stay true to the rate card. They consider your ride history, location, destination, and time of day. They even factor in how much charge your phone has when determining the cost of your ride. Leaving a gated community to head to a five-star restaurant? Expect your ride to cost more than someone going from their apartment building to the Dollar General.

Wait! You may be wondering . . . why does battery life matter? At the end of the night, someone with a fully charged phone is less desperate. That person will wait instead of taking a higher fare. On the other hand, people who are worried about their phone dying will take the higher fare to ensure they get a ride before their phone dies.

Two passengers could request the exact same trip simultaneously and get two different prices. It is all determined by algorithms.

Uber used to allow drivers to see customer fares in the app, but now they follow Lyft's policy. Drivers are no longer permitted to see what passengers pay for rides. When I compared customer fares at the end of a ride, Uber sometimes took seventy percent of the total charge. Other times, the company took a loss. Why intentionally take a loss on a ride? The algorithm. It tells execs that those little losses here and there assure brand loyalty. Use Uber daily, weekly, or monthly, and the company will take a loss on one ride to ensure you use them over and over.

Ever wondered why Uber shows your driver's location on a map and why there's a running countdown to when they should arrive instead of just saying what time the driver will show up? It would have been simpler to build an app without these features. But picturing the driver moving across a map, essentially racing against the clock, is a psychological ploy to make the waiting experience more pleasant. After all, what's the worst part of anything? Ask Tom Petty, and you'll get the right answer: the waiting. Watching the car battle the countdown keeps you engaged and distracted, making the waiting not so bad after all.

Have you ever noticed that your available Uber choices aren't always the same? If the algorithm decides you're a cost-conscious consumer, you'll see the lowest price option first. Enjoy luxury rides? Uber Black or Uber Comfort might top the list. Impatient? Quickest available will always greet you inside the app. These are just a few subtle ways Uber manipulates you to keep using the app.

Allowing customers to rate drivers is another manipulative tool. Uber rates drivers on their last 500 passenger ratings, so your rating has a mathematically insignificant impact on driver rating. Also, there's no lower limit to driver ratings that automatically deactivates a driver. So, rage on with your one-star reviews. It won't sink your driver's career. It simply gives you a false sense of control in your experience.

#UberProTip—Download both the Lyft and Uber apps. Prices for rides vary tremendously, and you can often find a quicker or cheaper ride by checking both apps.

BEAUFORT, BLACK CARDS & THE WATER FESTIVAL

"Dude, you've got to turn around. I left my black card with a stripper!"—Drunken Golfer

#UberProTip—If you aren't going to tip your driver, don't tell him you'll tip on the app. Admitting you're cheap is better than being cheap and dishonest.

The bulk of my rides were given in and around Beaufort, South Carolina. Its historic downtown sits on a picturesque bluff lined with oak trees draped with Spanish moss blowing in the wind. While driving down Bay Street toward the historic district, you pass beautifully maintained homes, some centuries old, and sailboats moored in the marina. It's easy to see why the town was settled in the early eighteenth century. Today, it's a quiet, sleepy little town on the intercoastal waterway, the gateway to South Carolina's other barrier islands.

FIVE STAR RIDES

Everyone headed to vacation on St. Helena Island, Harbor Island, Hunting Island, or Fripp Island passes through Beaufort on their way in and out of town. Retirees, magazine writers, and travel website owners love Beaufort. Year after year, it's consistently rated as one of the United States' best small towns and travel destinations. Beautiful waterways, historic charm, and hard-working community leaders ensure it's a great place for people to retire or vacation.

Speaking of community leaders, they love festivals. They host a monthly event downtown, and nearly every crustacean in the ocean has its own weekend festival. The Oyster Festival coincides with Restaurant Week. That's followed by the Soft-Shell Crab Festival and then Shrimp Festival.

Folks in Beaufort County also love to drink. It ranks among the top counties in South Carolina for alcohol consumption. This is probably related to how much time folks spend on the beach and in the water. Once the weather warms up, the boat landings stay full every weekend until the weather gets too cold to spend the day boating.

While the local sandbars and crustacean festivals draw crowds, the main event is the annual Water Festival. A ten-day event in the July heat, the Water Festival is a ten-night party. For nearly two full weeks, the park downtown by the river gets fenced off for concerts and dances. The area pulsates nightly with teenagers, young adults, middle-aged folks, and senior citizens.

Friday night, the opening ceremony includes fireworks and sets the stage for the next day of chaos. The first Saturday of Water Festival features the biggest concert act of the event. It usually sells out, and downtown is packed the entire night.

A few years ago, some locals hosted a concert on the sandbar in Beaufort River across from downtown Beaufort on Water Festival's opening Saturday afternoon. It stuck. While not an official Water Festival event, the concert draws thousands of people in boats and has exponentially increased the craziness of Water Festival opening weekend. People come into town for Water Festival, but the younger sandbar crowd starts drinking around 10 a.m. and doesn't stop 'til last call or they pass out.

In the first year of the concert, I talked my way on to a boat to experience the madness, but as a local high school teacher, I figured it was a bad idea to be surrounded by rampant underage drinking. So, I've never been back to the sandbar during Water Festival.

For 355 days a year, Beaufort rideshare passengers are pretty chill. Most rides are not memorable. Starting the first Saturday of the Water Festival, that goes out the window. Passengers get younger, more entitled, and dangerously intoxicated. I've never been berated so often or had passengers act so belligerently as on Water Festival Saturday night. If you've followed the Murdaugh drama here in the lowcounty, picture a car full of kids like "Timmy." That's your typical Saturday night ride during Water Festival.

Of course, early drinking means daytime behavior isn't that much better. Many passengers will start the day on boats, causing a surge of marina pickups during the late afternoon as they transition from the sandbar to downtown. Marina rides are typically more trouble than they're worth. The rides are short, and there's an overabundance of drunk frat bros. Hence why I stopped taking these gigs during Water Festival after two years of experience. One special bro wanted to fight me. (I tell that story in the final chapter, "Zero Fs Given.")

While that dude took it to the extreme, the typical Water Festival Saturday starts by picking up shoeless, shirtless, carefree passengers. As the day progresses, it transitions into ever-increasing versions of drunk and disorderly until culminating in late-night debauchery. Piling onto their antics, late-night passengers lose their ability to do math. At the end of the night, passengers often try fitting more people into my vehicle than I can legally carry or they paid for. Driving a larger vehicle exacerbates this issue, as people order a four-seat ride and beg you to allow six to save a couple bucks.

I sympathize with passengers who are exploited by the rideshare companies' ridiculous late-night fares. However, you don't hurt the company by shortchanging your driver.

NOT DRIVING DIANA

One Saturday night Water Festival ride was particularly memorable.

It was just after midnight when my phone dings for a fairly long ride to a golf community outside of Beaufort. It was a regular ride request: four passengers and the cheapest available fare. It paid well, but it took me about an hour to pick up the passengers, get them to their destination, and return downtown for the next surge ride.

As I pulled over on Bay Street outside of Luther's, I saw a large, drunk throng of people moving toward me. That was the first sign of trouble. I rolled down my window and tried to identify Clay, my passenger. Instead of Clay, a very intoxicated, older woman approached unsteadily. She'd clearly had a long day and night.

"Uuuuuuber," she slurred.

I explained that I'm looking for Clay, and she slapped her hand on my door.

"I'm Diana," she yelled, "but thassss usss."

Now I had a real problem. There were at least seven in the group, and I couldn't get all of them in my vehicle. I contemplated canceling the ride and driving away, but instead attempted to convince Diana that there were too many people for my vehicle and the type of ride she ordered.

Initially, she was stunned. Then she started counting seats and insisted they could squeeze in. I calmly explained it doesn't work that way. I couldn't carry more passengers than I had seat belts, and I wouldn't take more passengers than she paid for.

Diana then did what I expected. She started ranting and raving, cursing me and Uber and my "stupid, ugly Jeep."

As her drunk crew realized what was happening, her even more drunk daughter stumbled over and started repeating her mother's cursing and insults word for word. After soaking up the tag-team creativity a while, I drove away, only to wind up stuck because another rideshare driver was trying to back up down a narrow, one-way street. Not sure if she was confused, drunk, or stupid, but she seemed bent on wasting even more of my time.

Had the next ride gone poorly, I might have called it a night and abandoned my pursuit of a $1,000 weekend. Instead, the stars aligned with the algorithm. Every ride the rest of the night was either entertaining or a financial winner, a heaping helping of karma after drunk Diana and her drunker daughter.

My first ride request after drunk Diana was less than half a mile away. The ride was shorter, the passenger sober, and the pay more than made up for the ride I just lost. Added bonus: the sober passenger gave my biggest tip of the night.

For the rest of the night, every pickup came from Luther's or Q on Bay. Hilariously, every time I went back, drunk Diana and her drunker daughter were still on the curb, waiting for a ride home.

As luck had it, my last ride of the night was around 1:30 a.m. It was for two couples I picked up earlier in the day. They were part of the no-shoes, no-shirts, no-problems crowd, and they were feeling no pain. They were stoked to get the same driver a second time, and as they struggled with their seat belts, I told them about drunk Diana. Giggling like drunk school children, these two couples suggested we drive by Diana and say how much they enjoyed riding with me. It took Diana and her crew a few seconds to register what was happening, but once they did, they gave the expected response. Somehow, Diana and her daughter leapt to their feet, unloaded a full volley of profanity, and offered us an enthusiastic double-bird salute.

CREDIT-WORTHY RIDE HOME

On another Water Festival Saturday night, I caught a surge from Beaufort that took me to Hilton Head. Typically, I wouldn't want such a long ride during Water Festival. I could make better money staying in town. But since this was a surge ride and I was being paid double, I took it.

While in Hilton Head, I took a couple of rides there. Then I got lucky—my phone alerted me that someone needed a ride back toward Beaufort. This was the best-case scenario. I was going to essentially get paid for driving home. My excitement lessened when I noticed my pickup was waiting at Centerfolds, Beaufort County's only gentleman's club. Drive for Uber or Lyft long, and you quickly learn to dread strip-club pickups. These pickups inevitably involve a full car of wasted guys who are loud and reek of beer and desperation. Icing on the cake: they usually don't tip.

Though less than excited, the ride would take me home. So, I rolled up looking for Jimmy. A group of typical strip-club guys emerged, waving their phones at me. There were four older guys who flew in for a weekend of golf, beer, and—well, strippers. Thankfully, they were nice enough and had been drinking in moderation, so they were relatively coherent. It wound up being a nice, easy ride back to a golf club between Hilton Head and Beaufort. Despite picking them up at a strip club, I was fairly confident the ride would result in a good tip since golfers, caddies, bartenders, and servers are reliable tippers.

Soon as we paid the toll on the Cross Island Parkway, Jimmy jerked upright in the passenger seat. His face went pale.

"Guys," he said, "I left my credit card back there—with Cinnamon."

Instead of leaving his credit card overnight with Cinnamon at Centerfolds, I turned around, paid the toll a second time, and drove to the club to retrieve his credit card. The whole time, Jimmy thanked me over and over.

He promised he would make it worth my while. Granted, I didn't believe him, but it was a surge ride, and I didn't mind keeping the meter running.

This was in the good old days when Uber used multipliers for surge pricing. If the ride was a 2.0, you got paid double the normal rate. During big events, I've seen the multiplier hit 10.0 for a brief period. Unfortunately, this incentive no longer exists for drivers. The rideshare companies use multipliers to upcharge passengers during high demand, but they don't pass any of the extra cash along to drivers. But more on that later.

Anyway, we get back to the club, and Jimmy jumps out to retrieve the card. While he's inside looking for the card, his buddies roast him, hypothesizing what Cinnamon used his card to buy during our journey. Soon enough, Jimmy reemerges, card in hand. This time, we make the trip without incident.

I parked outside of their condo, and everyone filed out of the car. Jimmy came to the driver side window to thank me again.

"I really appreciate it," he said. Then he backed it up by pulling out a roll of cash. He peeled off five twenties. "That do for a tip?"

I nodded and thanked him, then left with my first $100 tip. It wasn't the last time I got a $100 tip from someone leaving Centerfolds, but that's a story for another chapter. Skip to "You've Got to Be Kidding Me" if you can't wait to hear it.

#UberProTip—Don't leave your black card with a stripper. But if you do, a $100 tip will get you VIP service from your Uber driver—even if it didn't from Cinnamon.

CHARLESTON & CANCELLATION RATES

"I don't have to ride with you."
"Nah, buddy, you don't get to ride with me."

#UberProTip—Your Uber driver cannot drive your eight-year-old for school. If the driver is willing, don't let your child ride with him.

Charleston is one of my favorite cities in the world. I never get tired of visiting. I love the Battery, Folly, Sullivan's, IOP, and the food. I don't think I've ever been to Charleston and not dreamed of living there. Minus the traffic, there's not a single bad thing to say about Charleston.

That said, I've never enjoyed driving in Charleston. I'm not wired for urban rideshare driving. The combination of traffic, difficult pickups and drop-offs, and short rides makes it an unpleasant experience. But much like driving in

Savannah, there's money to be made there. So if I find myself in Charleston, I make the best of it.

One reason Charleston is a difficult place to drive is because you never know what you'll get from a ride. The metro area sprawls endlessly, which can land you a long way from where you want to be with a single ride. A ride from downtown might take you two blocks, across the bridge to Mount Pleasant, to a beach, or out of town and away from the money. Staying in town ups your chances of making money, but even that comes with headaches.

I tried late-night Charleston driving a couple times, but I never braved the last-call shift. Charleston is just too far from Beaufort to attempt the ride home at 3 a.m. I got into a nice rhythm in the beach towns a couple of times and did well, but my preferred routine was to take someone to the airport, catch random rides for an hour or two, and then cruise back to Beaufort.

I once drove a taxi driver home who went drinking at a strip club. The guy got so drunk he couldn't do what he got paid to do and needed me to drive him home. This was funny, but the ride wasn't. He told me a pair of the vilest stories I've ever heard. And no, I'm not printing them. He absolutely refused to stop talking. I cranked the radio to attempt to drown him out, but he wouldn't take the hint. He just kept blabbing.

CANCELED CONNECTION

Another frustrating aspect of Charleston driving is that no rider is ever ready for their ride. It doesn't matter where I picked them up, I'd have to wait on the passenger when

I arrived—assuming I could find them. Finding a parking place in downtown is almost impossible. City officials make it even more difficult by banning late-night pickups on certain downtown streets.

This connection difficulty leads to a lot of canceled rides. That's a problem. Remember—rideshare companies need drivers to accept every ride they're offered. Canceling an offered and accepted ride is a cardinal sin. To limit your transgressions, Uber and Lyft use all forms of manipulation and intimidation. First is the carrot. They offer you status and rewards if you maintain an extraordinarily high acceptance rate and an extraordinarily low cancellation rate. Then comes the stick.

Lyft bombards you with emails and messages when you decline or cancel rides. If you still don't fall into lockstep, they hit you with thirty-minute suspensions from taking rides.

Uber takes a more psychological approach. They work super hard to convince you that being a gold, diamond, or platinum driver is worth it. Ideally, this is enough to get you to accept and complete all rides on your own. But if that doesn't work, they will send you a message: "It looks like you aren't accepting rides right now, so we are signing you out of your account." Signing back into your account is a real hassle. You have to pull over, stop driving, and go back through the log-in process instead of just turning the app on.

Why do they do this? To allow as many people as possible to use their service. People don't like waiting, and drivers who decline or cancel rides make them do just that. And if someone is stuck waiting for Uber, she may try Lyft or vice-versa. The company makes more money when drivers accept and complete more rides. It seems reasonable enough, right? This is the problem though. While it's good for rideshare companies, it's not good for drivers. We aren't employees. We're independent contractors. Rideshare companies spend millions each year to keep it that way. But independent contractors usually have the option to accept or decline work without penalty. What independent contractor voluntarily accepts jobs they don't want or won't make any money? Rideshare companies use acceptance rates/cancellation rates to extract the benefits of employees without paying the higher cost of having employees.

NO, THANK YOU

So, why don't drivers want to accept all rides? For many reasons. Originally, neither Uber nor Lyft told drivers where they were going before starting a trip. That meant you could drive twenty minutes out of town to pick someone up for a minimum-fare ride. When this happened, you'd drive thirty minutes, make $2.62 (minus expenses), and wind up twenty minutes away from your next ride. You could easily spend more in gas than you make on fares. Because of that, many drivers don't pick up passengers more than ten minutes away.

Why would a driver cancel a ride? Again, so many reasons! There may be too many passengers, unaccompanied underage passengers, dangerously intoxicated passengers, or passengers who leave you waiting for ten minutes. Neither rideshare company differentiates cancellations. Cancel for any reason, and it registers the same way.

I canceled one ride when someone wanted me to drive

their unaccompanied eight-year-old child. I rolled up to the apartment, and out strolls a pigtailed second grader with a pink book bag slung across her shoulders. I rolled down my window and asked to talk to her mom. Mom comes out and is legitimately pissed that I won't drive her daughter to school alone and insists other drivers will.

That wasn't a one-time thing. On multiple other occasions, I've canceled rides when parents wanted me to drive infants and toddlers without car seats.

Uber and Lyft both claim that cancellation fees get paid out automatically after waiting for the prescribed amount of time and canceling. The companies also allow you to cancel to protect your safety or avoid participating in illegal or company policy-violating activities. Or so they say. Nice as it sounds, it ain't true. About a quarter of the time, I have to stop and call or message the support team to persuade them to pay out the cancellation fee. Most of the time, Uber eventually pays, but as will be discussed in a later chapter, Lyft goes to extraordinary lengths to avoid paying cancellation fees.

One of my funniest cancellations occurred at Slightly North of Broad, a popular downtown restaurant. A passenger requested a ride, then accidentally moved the pin to another location. I waited at the pin for a few minutes, then called the passenger instead of canceling and charging them a cancellation fee. When the guy answered, he started berating me for making him wait. I tried explaining what happened, but he wanted to hear none of it. Once he finished ranting, he told me where he was.

When I arrived, he waltzed into the street, drink in hand.

He forcefully knocked on my window before I could get the car in park. I rolled the window down, and he told me through liquor-loosened lips that he wasn't ready yet. His wife was still waiting to pay the tab. I started explaining that I'd already waited a long time for him, and the only reason I didn't cancel already was out of courtesy. This didn't settle well with the guy. So, he launched into a profanity-laced tirade about not having to ride with me.

I interrupted to correct him.

"You don't get to ride with me."

He gave me a confused look, as I hit the cancel button on the app and drove off.

Pleased with myself, I moved up a couple of parking spots to wait for my next ride. It didn't take long. And guess who my next ride request was from? If you guessed angry drunk guy I just left, you're right. Since I have a particular taste for passive-aggressive revenge, I accepted the ride.

Mr. Angry Drunk was well past the point of exhibiting any higher-order thinking skills, so I waited another five minutes for him to come to the car. He never figured out I was waiting for him though. Once my waiting timer hit zero, I canceled the ride, pocketed another cancellation fee, then drove far enough away avoid the guy the rest of the night.

#UberProTip—Don't get angry at your driver if you enter the wrong pickup location and are too drunk to realize it. Rideshare drivers are there to serve, but being belligerent lowers the chance they will go out of their way to help you.

DITCHES, DRUNKS & DENTS

"C'mon, man—at least close the door behind you."

#UberProTip—Don't order your Uber before you close your tab and expect the driver to wait on you. Wait-time fees are pennies, and your driver's time is worth more that.

While intoxicated passengers are an everyday occurrence in the life of a rideshare driver, we don't encounter disappearing passengers. Not normally at least.

The worst riders are always the result of a Good Samaritan ordering a ride for someone who's too drunk to order a ride for themselves. It's certainly better than letting a drunk person drive themselves home; however, these rides are at best a headache and at worst a harrowing event for the driver.

After a few years of late-night rides, I stopped driving solo drunks. I only transported drunk passengers with someone to ensure they got out of the car and into their homes.

LAUGHING ... SOMETIMES

Sometimes it was funny.

One lady made me pull over repeatedly on the way to her Parris Island home. Soon as we weren't moving, she was out on the shoulder, vomiting. I mentioned that I knew her neighbors. She begged me not to mention the ride to her neighbors, then tipped me $20 as hush money.

My first St. Patrick's Day rider was a man who couldn't make it to his house. Instead, he climbed into his truck bed to sleep off his revelry.

Other times, the drunkenness isn't so funny—at least not in the moment.

WHERE'D HE GO?

The vanishing passenger started off blandly. I pulled up to his house and found someone standing in the driveway, waiting. This is usually a good sign. It means the passengers are sober enough to follow me on the app and polite enough not to make me wait. However, the man in the driveway wasn't getting a ride. He ordered the ride for a drunk friend. I soon realized this was a very good thing. But in the moment, it was disappointing.

I rolled my eyes. Here we go again.

Eventually, the passenger emerged unsteadily from the house, a plastic bag of beers in hand. My heart dropped. He nearly fell down the steps, stumbled toward me, and banged his bag of beers against the door as his friend helped him work the handle.

It was a short ride, and his friend pre-tipped me in cash, so off we went.

The ride was uneventful since drunk dude was on the verge of passing out the whole time. As we arrived at drunk rider's destination, my app pinged another ride for me. I focused on my next passenger while drunk dude exited the car. When I looked up, my passenger was gone, but he left my door wide open. I sighed. C'mon man, I thought, at least close the door behind you.

More than a little annoyed, I exited the car to close the door. Then I realized why I didn't see the passenger walk away and why he didn't close the door. He was passed out in the ditch next to his driveway. I called his name and gently punched his shoulder. It was no use. He was out cold.

I called his friend who ordered the ride. At first the friend didn't seem concerned. But when I said I was going to call 911, he became troubled and promised to take care of things.

A few minutes later, the drunk guy's roommates came out of the house to tend to their friend. Once they arrived, I left the passed-out passenger in the ditch and in their care.

MVP SAVES AND MISTAKES

Unsurprisingly, drunk people aren't the best with balance. The dude who fell in the ditch isn't the only passenger who lost in a showdown with gravity after a night out.

I once drove a lady home in Hilton Head who insisted on riding shotgun. She was highly intoxicated, and when we arrived at her home, she fell out of the car and onto the asphalt. Fortunately, the ground wasn't far from the seat of my Civic, and all that was injured was her pride and dignity.

Another time, a husband proved to be the real ride MVP, saving his wife from what could have been a serious injury. I could tell she was drunk-drunk, and her husband was aware of this as well. While riding in the backseat of my larger, farther-from-the-ground SUV, the husband repeatedly reminded his wife to let him help her out of the car when they got home. Well, she refused to listen.

When we pulled up to their house, she opened the door to exit. Unfortunately, she didn't have a clean dismount. She fell face first toward the driveway as her husband rounded the corner. Somehow, he caught her before she hit the ground. Definitely the most clutch save I've seen in all my 10,000 rides.

Balance problems don't always result in laughs though. Sometimes it leads to blood or body shops.

I often picked up people who were so dangerously intoxicated that they barely made it to my car. These excessively drunk folks are the usual suspects: college students, bachelorettes, golf bros, etc. But they aren't the only ones who drink themselves into oblivion.

I was driving through the back of a wealthy island enclave near Charleston toward a swanky exclusive gala. The local elites don black ties and their fanciest adult prom dresses. Cocktail hour is followed by dinner parties and then the main event.

This is the place to see and be seen, to gossip about and gawk at whatever has the locals aflutter at the moment. The event is ostensibly a benefit, but from what I gathered from passengers, the evening's true pleasure is gossiping and emptying wine bottles.

As the party winds down, the event location becomes a regular late-night pickup point, shuttling people from the $150-per-ticket event back to their waterfront homes where they left their Mercedes-Benzes and Range Rovers.

The good ones didn't make me wait long. They even threw in a small tip for getting them home safely. But most of the time, the tip was smaller than I'd get from the Sleep Inn housekeeper or Waffle House waitress. The bad ones used every second of the seven minutes Uber requires drivers to wait before canceling the ride becomes an option.

SLIPPING AND TIPPING

I once had a dolled-up lady enter the car and declare she was waiting on her husband. No big deal—annoying, but it happens all the time. As the timer closed in on zero, I asked if her husband was coming. She looked me dead in the face.

"He just got another drink, so he'll probably be a few minutes," she said. "But you get paid to wait, so we'll just wait on him."

In an utterly shocking turn of events for her, I wasn't going to wait while her absent husband finished his drink. I explained Uber's wait-time and cancellation policy. She took the news rather poorly and became the 757th drunk passenger to inform me that she would be "speaking with Uber in the morning," and that I should "prepare myself to be fired."

(That reminds me of another confused passenger. I drove her from the Marina in downtown Beaufort to Publix. Once there, she expected me to wait outside while she went grocery shopping and then to drive her back to the Marina. She, too, was baffled that her $7 ride didn't entitle her to an hour of my time.)

But back to the point of this story. Because the booze started flowing at cocktail hour, many in the crowd are in desperate need of a ride home by ten that evening. Close to midnight, riders either know how to pace themselves or should have stopped drinking hours ago. Enter the star of our show.

She staggered out of the building, making her way toward the car with her husband's assistance. I grimaced, expecting the worst as she approached a set of stairs in high heels. Fortunately, her husband sensed the danger and had her lose the heels before attempting the stairs. Thanks to his quick thinking, they avoided danger—momentarily.

At the car, the husband acted as a gentleman. He opened the rear passenger door for his wife, but he lacked the athletic ability and foresight to prevent what happened next. While the husband opened the rear door for his wife, she decided to sit in the front instead. She stepped around him to grab the handle of the front door, and disaster struck.

She either forgot about the small step down from the curb or was incapable of navigating it. Either way, she fell headlong, and I saw the whole thing. I watched in slow motion as gravity remained undefeated and she cracked her head on my headlights. Bob Dylan sang "Blood on the Tracks." My song would have been "Blood on the Headlights."

Fortunately, there was no serious damage to the diva or to my car. They quickly mended her bloody forehead and folded her into the backseat, where she laid down, forcing the husband to ride up front with me.

Mercifully, the ride home was short and silent as the car filled with the overwhelming smell of alcohol and embarrassment. Surprisingly, that ride ended with a pretty significant tip. I think hubby was pretty happy that I agreed to take his ballerina home after a less-than-graceful entrance to my vehicle.

FAREWELL, BOB

Back in Beaufort, it was time for a regular customer, Bob. I'm pretty sure Bob was a functional alcoholic. I drove him to and from bars so regularly that I got to know him as a person. He had a pretty good blue-collar job and always went to the bar early—before dinner—and never stayed out late. I suspected this allowed him to get drunk with enough time to sleep it off for work the next day.

Bob was a nice enough guy, and he always tipped on the app (although tips from the rides home always came the next day). One night when I took Bob home, it was clear he'd gone harder than normal in the bars. I didn't really think anything of it. Bob was a big boy and never caused any trouble. To that point, he was a nearly perfect customer—always ready for pickups, good taste in music, always tipped.

I didn't know it, but this was the next-to-last time I would ever drive Bob.

When we made it back to his house, Bob rolled out of the car unsteadily and ambled toward the door. He took one step, staggered, and then righted himself. Another sideways step, another stagger, and another righting. Realizing he was in trouble, he attempted to steady himself on my car, but he misjudged the distance, and down he went. Fortunately for Bob—but unfortunately for me, he crashed forehead first into the front panel of my car. I got out to check on him, but by the time I reached him, he'd gathered himself and was on the way to his house. The next day when I saw my car in the daylight, a head-shaped dent in my quarter panel looked back at me.

Damn it, Bob!

For a normal passenger, I'd take pictures, send a damage report to Uber, and hope for some reimbursement. But I liked Bob. I felt sorry for him. And knew it wouldn't be long before I picked him up again. We'd talk about it then, like men, and he would do the right thing.

I was right. A couple days later, I got pinged to pick Bob up from home. I showed him the damage he did on his last ride. His memory of that night was foggy, but he didn't dispute it and promised to make it right. Then he took my phone number and said he would put me in touch with a guy—his guy—to fix it.

The rest of the trip, we casually conversed. Like I'd done so many times before, I dropped him off at Brody's, his bar of choice. Then Bob did something he'd never done before. He gave me a one-star rating, and I never drove Bob again. And of course, he never put me in touch with his guy to fix my car.

This is why rideshare drivers can't make exceptions for their customers. Once I realized Bob was flaking on me, I submitted the pictures and damage claim to Uber Support. True to form, they replied that the passenger said he didn't do it, leaving me with the bill for his drunken damage.

#UberProTip—Don't get so drunk you fall out of your ride and into a ditch.

56

EXPENSES & AN EXPLANATION

"A man never knows quite how much he has to be thankful for until he has to pay taxes on it."—Anonymous

One of the first things you learn as a rideshare driver is that what you make in the app isn't actually what you make. Cash out your weekly earnings and add that amount to your monthly budget, and you'll be in for a world of hurt down the road. That's why tips are so important. A $2 tip on a $10 ride only increases the passenger's trip cost by twenty percent. However, it increases driver earnings on that ride by as much as fifty percent. Why? Because Uber and Lyft often pay out less than half of the fare for shorter rides.

Let's say you put in twelve hours on Friday and Saturday nights and bring in $300, including tips. That averages to $25 an hour—a pretty good weekend, right? Not so fast. A huge chunk of that $300 gets accounted for before you get paid. Rideshare companies don't deduct taxes, but you still gotta pay them. As a result, approximately $45 of that $300 goes straight to Uncle Sam. Rides come in all shapes and sizes, but twelve hours of driving will require at least one tank of gas. That's a minimum of $60. Now, you're down to $195 for twelve hours of work—a little over $16 per hour.

Then there's wear and tear on your vehicle. A night of driving puts you twelve hours closer to your next oil change and tire replacement. Being conservative, you should save at least ten percent of your gross income to cover belts, hoses, brakes, and all the other car maintenance items needed to keep your car on the road and earning money. You're now down to $165 (less than $14 an hour).

But wait—there's more! After a weekend of driving, you probably need to drop some cash to clean your car or risk getting lower ratings and fewer tips for driving a dirty car. And what about snacks? You'll get hungry and thirsty during your shift. Subtract these expenses, and you may barely clear $12 an hour.

What happens if you don't take expenses into account on a weekly basis? You get a massive bill from Uncle Sam in April or scramble for $1,000 for tires or another unexpected repair. And don't forget to set aside $1,000 in case of an accident. Uber and Lyft provide insurance that covers you while driving for them, but the policy has a $1,000 deductible. So, get in an accident with an uninsured or underinsured driver, and you are on the hook for $1,000 before the company pitches in a penny.

But tires, gas, taxes, and car washes aren't the only regular expenses. When passengers borrow your phone charger and forget to give it back, you have to buy a new one. Stocking up on air freshener helps prevent one-star ratings from riders who climb in after hygienically challenged passengers.

As you can see, it doesn't take long for the list of expenses to pile up. The bulk of my rideshare driving took place in a 2016 Honda Civic. It was the perfect car for the gig—low maintenance, good gas mileage, and easy to navigate in tight spaces. There was only one problem. Driving 30,000 miles a year on South Carolina roads destroyed my tires. In five years, I went through nearly a dozen new tires on my Civic. Normal wear and tear, nails, potholes, and curbs all claimed tires. If there was something sharp with the potential to puncture a tire, I found it in my Civic.

At this point, you may wonder why anyone would drive for a rideshare company. If the companies aren't driver friendly and customers are difficult, why drive longer than absolutely necessary? The key factors that ensure a steady supply of drivers are marketing and sheer desperation.

Rideshare companies constantly advertise the many benefits of driving. These campaigns feature promises of high hourly wages in combination with the freedom of being your own boss. They also offer some amazing sign-on bonuses for new drivers and any drivers who convince someone else to drive. For many people, driving for a rideshare company is the best job they can find. For others, it's a convenient second source of income. Drivers are in charge of their own schedule, and there are no language barriers or scheduling conflicts.

What about me? Why do I keep driving? After more than 10,000 rides, my reasons are similar to those above, but there are layers. For me, rideshare driving offers an additional stream of income that provides the opportunity to earn money while maintaining control of my schedule. Because rideshare income has never been my primary income, I've used it to fund family vacations and travel experiences. It fits into my schedule and works for me and my family. If the rides are worth it and I want to drive forty hours a week, I do. If I want to work for an hour, I can. If I don't want to open the apps for two weeks, I don't. There's no pressure.

Because I'm not beholden to a boss, a clock, or a calendar, I can pursue other ventures and travel when the opportunity arrives.

And while the pages of this book are filled with the most interesting or awful rides and riders I've encountered, most of my 10,000 rides were simple transactions or enjoyable experiences.

#UberProTip—To always find a driver when you need one, tip well. Most Uber drivers quit driving in less than a year because it doesn't make financial sense to continue.

FEBREZE, FIREBALL & FIVE STARS

"I will drink Fireball here or there. I will drink Fireball everywhere."—Uber Passenger with Delusions of Being the Next Dr. Seuss

One of a rideshare driver's best friends is his trusty bottle of Febreze. It sucked wearing masks during the COVID-19 pandemic, but it had one fringe benefit. Wearing a mask prevented me from being overpowered by the smells of passengers.

Drivers encounter all sorts of sight and sounds, and—believe it or not—scents. I'm not talking about an occasional whiff of something strange. I'm talking about I-can't-wait-to-finish-this-ride-because-this-joker-is-stank kinda stink. I can't tell you how many times I've had to finish a ride, roll all four windows down, pull over, and spray the car down before picking up the next passenger. I always keep Febreze within reach, so the next passenger doesn't blame me for the smells lingering from the last passenger. Some nights, I drive all the way home with my windows down to avoid trapping the funk in my car overnight.

Sources of the most common smells dealt with by rideshare drivers include:

1. Bad hygiene. Some people just don't take care of themselves properly. They don't brush their teeth or shower or wear deodorant or—well, you get the picture.

2. Beer. Whether passengers spill it on themselves or have it working its way out of their pores, it can give a car a brewery-esque odor.

3. Food. Leftovers and twelve-hour shifts in the kitchen transform the backseat into what smells like a seafood buffet.

4. Smoke. When the rider gets that last drag before climbing in, Febreze must come to the rescue once again.

5. Illegal Smoke. Prior to driving rideshare, I had no idea how many people get high before reporting to work. Some riders smoked so much I feared a contact high. I've got more to say about this—so much that it gets its own chapter later.

Bad smells are so common that Uber passengers who smell good are literally a breath of fresh air. Their entrance tempts me to comment on their nice odor. However, exclaiming, "Wow! You smell good" would be super creepy. So, I just enjoy the smell quietly.

While I keep a bottle of Febreze in my car, I don't keep a fully stocked bar in the trunk. Nor am I a member of the South Carolina Alcoholic Beverage Commission. You'd think at least one of those was true with the amount of drunkenness I'm exposed to while driving.

Passengers are often so inebriated that their attempts at conversation only make sense if you're equally drunk. These conversations commonly feature the same comment or question on repeat. Passengers either forget what they've already said or feel the need to drunkenly emphasize whatever semi-coherent thing they got out. They often thank me seventeen times during an eight-minute ride for getting them home safely. Or they vow repeatedly to tip you on the app since they don't have any cash. As you would expect, there's an inverse relationship between telling me they'll tip me and actually doing it!

On one particular ride, I pulled up to a dive bar as three people emerged and walked unsteadily to my car. The male opened the rear door and helped two female passengers into the backseat. Then he told me to get them home safely. Before I pulled out of the parking lot, I learned why they required assistance getting into the car. They were hammered, but not ready to stop partying.

As I worked my way out of the tight, crowded parking lot, one passenger decided the backseat didn't suit her. So, she climbed into the front seat. I don't mind people sitting beside me. I just prefer they don't climb from the back to the front while I'm driving.

This particular lady wasn't just drunk and daring. She was handsy as well. For the remainder of the ride, she begged for one more shot of fireball. Every time she asked, she grabbed my arm and whined, "Just one more shotttt of Firrreeballl."

I'm not sure where in my Honda Civic she thought I kept a stash of Fireball, but no matter how many times I explained that I didn't have any, she kept asking.

Most passengers have ratings between 4.8 and 5.0. This high rating occurs because drivers are forced to rate every ride, and the quickest way to get to the next ride is to give every passenger five stars. Rate a passenger lower, and you've got to stop driving to explain why your passenger didn't deserve the default five stars. Usually this isn't worth the effort. So, unless you're a one-star passenger I never want to pick up again, I'll give you five stars. However, there are exceptions.

I've picked up passengers with sub-4.0 ratings. I can't imagine how awful a passenger must be to dip below the four mark, but a select few pull it off. As a driver, I rarely consider passenger ratings before accepting a ride. So in reality, passenger ratings have zero impact on passengers. Occasionally, I turn down a late-night ride for a passenger with a low rating, but that's the exception—not the rule.

Driver ratings are similar. Both Uber and Lyft offer perks to high-rated drivers, but to qualify for those perks you must have hit required acceptance and cancellation rates and volume. Because of this, simply being a highly rated driver comes with no benefit.

My rating always hovers around 4.9. In rideshare speak, that rating proves I tolerate a pretty high level of nonsense, but I don't silently suffer entitled fools. When a rider can't comprehend the difference in service level between a $7 Uber ride and a chauffeur or their sense of entitlement turns to condescension and disrespect, we aren't the best match.

While ratings are always anonymous, it doesn't take much to know which rides low ratings come from. I have come to expect a low rating when I don't allow someone to bring open containers of alcohol into the car. Riders give low ratings whenever they aren't allowed to do something illegal or that they didn't pay for. Example: A rider orders a regular ride but actually needs an XL ride or second car.

A recent ride combined the best of both worlds. They

ordered an UberX because it was cheaper. When I arrived, all six passengers (yes, that's more than they paid for) held open containers, and they expected to take those containers with them to their destination. I explained that I could only accommodate four passengers since that's what they paid for. I further explained that those open containers are illegal in a moving vehicle. Eventually, they decided that I should take four of them. The other two would order a second ride for the rest of the group. Seemed like a reasonable solution. Until I opened the app the next morning to a low rating. All because I refused to provide an illegal service they didn't pay for.

Fortunately, this is strictly a side hustle for me. That gives me the luxury of maintaining a low threshold of nonsense that I will tolerate. If rider behavior is bad, I will regularly close the app for the night. And if it comes to it, I don't fear being deactivated. There are other ways to make cash.

The meaninglessness of ratings is lost on some drivers and passengers though. Karens are quick to announce that you're getting a one-star rating. It's the best they can do since they can't complain to your manager. If I got $1 every time someone threatened me with a one-star rating, I could buy a lot of Febreze!

My favorite threats involve canceled rides. When one group member is ready to go, but the rest won't leave the bar, the timer is my master. When it hits zero, I cancel the ride and leave. Doing anything else doesn't make financial sense. Or when I arrive at the pick-up destination and the group wants to cram seven people in my Civic. Canceled. Granted, I could risk stuffing my car with extra people, but an expensive ticket for a $10 ride doesn't make sense either.

In both scenarios, I'm stuck explaining why I won't bend or break the rules for strangers. And they get pissed. Once they realize anger won't change my mind, they break out the big guns: the threat of a one-star rating. Unfortunately, they can't rate a driver for a canceled ride. This is one rideshare policy I appreciate. So, when they throw that threat my way, I chuckle, wish them luck, shift into drive, and ease off the brake.

#UberProTip—If you're pleasant and smell good, you'll always get a five-star passenger rating from your driver.

GOLFERS & GRANDPAS

"Did that go in? I wasn't watching, did it go in? I didn't see it, could you tell me if it went in?"—Happy Gilmore

Golf is big in the lowcountry. It's not unusual to pick up a group of guys who came to town to caddy or play golf. From Charleston to Savannah, the coast of South Carolina and Georgia is littered with grade-A courses. Caddies regularly split time between here and up north, chasing the weather and tips. When they're here, I often drive them to or from the course and around town.

Both groups have their own quirks, but they tip well and are usually not demanding. The biggest request they make is to hit a fast-food drive-thru on the way home. One caddy offered me a $10 tip to stop at Burger King at the end of a night. It wasn't a request I'd typically agree to, but he was paying for it and was a good customer. My man ordered two whoppers, some chicken nuggets, a large fry, a soda, and a milkshake. He dropped a twenty spot on an order for one at Burger King—not something I've seen before or since.

Some exclusive clubs arrange transportation for golfers,

but it isn't always available when they want it. So occasionally, I pick up a straggler who wanted to stay longer than the group. This is typically a quick, easy ride—but not always. Which brings me to this chapter's tip.

#UberProTip: If you can't tell me where you are or where you're going, I can't take you home.

TO THE STORY . . .

My phone pinged at the end of the night. Someone needed a ride coming from Bay Street. I wasn't far away, and it wasn't very crowded, so I took it. When I showed up, I parked on the street where the rider's pin indicated on the app, but no one was there. I waited a couple of minutes, then texted the passenger. No response. I waited a few more minutes and called him. No response. At the end of my wait time, I called a third time. He answers.

"Where are you?" I asked.

He didn't know, so he named a couple of places that aren't in Beaufort. I got him to describe what was around him. With his description, I realized he was at Hemingway's. I directed him up to Bay Street, where I could pick him up.

He stumbled his way to the car and fell into the backseat. The ride started uneventful. Then we arrived at the gated community across from his golf course. The guy can't remember the gate code. Fortuitously, I'd been in that community earlier that night and remembered the code. I punched it in, and we made it past the gate. Easy enough. But it was a foretaste of the rest of the drive.

A couple more turns, and we arrived at the address he entered in the app. I pulled into the driveway and come to a stop. With a confused look, he told me we weren't at the right house. I read off the address and showed him the map.

"Guess I entered the wrong address," he said.

I asked for the right address, and he didn't know it. But he insisted he would recognize it. I know this probably won't end well, but against my better judgment I went with his plan. I backed out of the wrong driveway and cruised the dark, poorly lit, tree-filled, gated neighborhood.

As I drove, my drunk-out-of-his-mind passenger insisted he could find the house. After ten minutes, it was clear he couldn't. I told him I couldn't keep doing this, so he offered me $20 to keep looking. I sighed and kept up the hunt for the elusive house.

Eventually, the efforts paid off.

"This is it!" he shouted as if he discovered Atlantis.

I pulled into the driveway that was eerily familiar. Yes, we ended up right back at the first house we pulled into. It just looked different in the dark. I laughed off the mistake and drove off as soon as he exited the car. I wasn't sticking around to make sure it was the right one after all.

AROUND-TOWN CADDIE

Some golfers want more control over their experience than you get through the rideshare companies. They're eager to get you off the app, so they can deal with you directly.

My favorite duo requested a ride on Thursday night. Soon as I accepted the ride, they called me with a proposal. Essentially, they wanted to hire me as their private driver for the weekend. All it involved was driving them to Beaufort and back a couple of times, then to the airport on Sunday.

This was like hitting the jackpot! It meant scheduled rides and fair pay for the weekend instead of waiting for whoever Uber might send me. In following the first rule of negotiation, I didn't give them a price upfront. Instead, I asked what their budget was for the weekend. Right on cue, they offered $300 at the completion of the first ride and $300 more when I dropped them off at the airport. Since I would have done the whole thing for $300, I accepted without a counteroffer.

Though they could have ghosted me and only paid the initial $300, they made good on their end of the deal, and the weekend went off without a hitch. That planted a seed in my mind. Perhaps going out on my own was a better move than being a long-time rideshare driver. COVID-19 interrupted that plan, but the idea took root.

AGING ISSUES

One of my most popular Facebook #UberProTips posts went like this:

If you order an Uber and a car stops in middle of road right in front of you AND that car has an Uber sticker AND that car is the exact same color, make, and model as the car that you were told was coming to pick you up AND the driver looks like the picture of the driver you were told would be picking you up AND that car has the same plate number you were given, THEN that car is indeed your Uber.

This post was written after I reached my limit with technologically challenged boomers. These fine folks consistently wasted minutes of my life debating whether I was their Uber driver. When I arrived to pick them up, they refused to use a single piece of information at their disposal to confirm I was indeed their driver. They even overlooked context clues, such as the fact that I parked in front of them and sat staring at them. With boomers, I would eventually roll my window down and state that I was their driver. Their inevitable answer: A) "What's my name?" or B) "Oh, good! We didn't want to get into the wrong car." Add in some alcohol, and it was painfully difficult for some people to process whether or not I was there to pick them up.

Elderly people presented a different set of problems. Many of them struggled to believe or understand they didn't have to pay at the end of the ride. They also couldn't comprehend that my GPS could get me to their destination without their verbal, turn-by-turn and lane-changing instructions.

Other generational issues were more cultural. I once picked up an elderly lady and a young woman. They were in town for a family wedding and had some early morning errands to run. Something happened during the short trip to inspire the old lady to out herself as a bona fide, old-school racist. She wasn't a vitriolic hood-wearing Klan member, but she was a product of a family and community that felt superior to everyone—especially those of other ethnicities. Mercifully, the ride was short. True to form, there was no tip. After all, the help doesn't get paid extra for being the help.

I didn't give the ride much thought until later that evening when I picked up an old man at the same location.

This was another short ride, but that's all I needed. From our brief interaction, I gathered two pieces of information. 1. He, too, was an unapologetic racist. 2. He was married to the racist grandma I drove earlier in the day. So, in a single day—in a matter of hours, I marked Racist Grandma and Racist Grandpa off my Uber driver bingo card.

#UberProTip—If you're too drunk to tell me where you are and where you're going, it's going to be very difficult for me to take you home.

HILTON HEAD ISLAND & THE HERITAGE

"The quiet turns to revelry as the sun burns away the spring. The coastline starts to sing with young and heartless. Hilton Head and the Hamptons, where the rich all go to die, and the young kids all get high to pass time."—Zach Bryan

A preface is due here. The Heritage Foundation does amazing work. They've donated $50 million to charity since 1987, including four-year college scholarships to 375 high school students. The golf tournament is a well-organized, hugely popular event. Because it's open to whoever has money, the Foundation and the golf club can't be blamed for the out-of-control behavior of people once they leave the tournament.

Disclaimer applied, the RBC Heritage golf tournament on Hilton Head Island is stacked with entitled bros, ditzy fake blondes, and grandfathers and grandmothers acting like they're in college.

While PGA Tour and Hilton Head Island may conjure images of power-walking grandmas and wine-sipping gentlemen yelling at tourists to stay off their lawns, that's not what you find during the RBC Heritage.

ENTITLED CRAZIES

In the days surrounding the event, the Island is full. Spectators wait all year for the event, and they quickly book all the available accommodations. Hotels, condos, and Airbnbs are all at max capacity. Even more people drive in from the surrounding areas to partake of the event.

When I drove at the event, I worked nonstop from 3 p.m. to 3 a.m. (Uber kicks you off the app when you work twelve hours without a break.) I drove Thursday, Friday, and Saturday nights. Thanks to surge pricing and drunk tipping, I make more driving that weekend than most months. You might think driving for $50 an hour is easy money, but nothing is easy during Heritage weekend.

First, there's the traffic. The Heritage is held at Harbor Town Golf Links in the rear of the Sea Pines gated community. Entering and exiting Sea Pines is a pain during tourist season. It's almost impossible during the Heritage tournament. There are more cars than roads in Hilton Head all spring and summer, but the Heritage gets them all pointed in the same direction. Even with tournament shuttles, traffic is a nightmare. No one can drive or navigate traffic circles on the island. Locals blame tourists, but bad driving in Hilton Head is a year-round epidemic.

Second, Hilton Head's entitlement reaches all the way to eleven during Heritage week. Overnight, rules only apply to the other guy. Don't like a policy or procedure? Ignore it or change it.

Case in point: the tournament designates a specific spot for rideshare pickups. It's convenient enough, but you have to walk to get to it. This makes the folks attending the Heritage rather angry. Every third or fourth rider cusses me for not driving past the road-closed signs to get them. Then there are the lectures I get on Saturday night when I explain that liquor stores are closed until Monday. The only thing that makes more people angry is when I tell people they can't bring their beer bottles or wine cups with them.

When tournament play ends for the day, the nightlife kicks into full gear. From an outsider's perspective, it seems many people in town for the tournament are more interested in the parties and debauchery.

Last call in South Carolina comes before 2 a.m., but the parties continue well past that, and picking up passengers at the end of the night is a full-contact sport. There are only a few spots open late on Hilton Head. As a result, most pickups come from a cluster of bars called The BarMuda Triangle. And you never know what you'll get there. You could pick up a group of girls with fake IDs on one ride, then a cluster of wine-drunk divorcees looking for a new man the next. Whoever you pick up, none of them can read the description of your car or plate number. And navigating the parking lot to pick them up is enough to qualify drivers for American Ninja Warriors.

Unfortunately, our forefathers who designed The BarMuda Triangle parking lots did so with little foresight. While full of drunks, the parking lots are not designed for a mass exodus of drunk people. Getting in and out without hitting a pedestrian or another vehicle requires maximum focus and concentration. You quickly learn that the drunk golf bro staring at you will absolutely step in front of you at the last second. You also realize that every drunk person doesn't call an Uber at the end of the night. Some try to drive themselves home. When they do, they back up their car while you wait for your passenger to close the door so you can get out of the way. You also need sharpened verbal skills to effectively communicate that your name is not Charlie, you aren't driving an Isuzu Rodeo, and the guy who pissed himself is trying to get into the wrong vehicle.

Because you're constantly busy, no ride is boring. When you check the app to see how you made out at the end of the night, you realize you had a good week in a single night, so the chaos is worth it. Oh, and the stories—they're gold! Some made it into other chapters, and others are so strange they ascend beyond the written word.

Outside of Heritage week, Hilton Head is one of my favorite places to drive. It's way better than Charleston or Savannah and more lucrative than staying close to home. With some notable exceptions, most rides are pleasant, and the tips are good on Hilton Head. Why? Everyone is happy to be there. Whether there for a conference, golf getaway, or family vacation, almost everyone I drive on Hilton Head is having a good time. The deciding factor for ride quality is whether the passenger had too much of a good time.

Recently, I rolled up to a bar just after 7 p.m. as Javier, a newly minted twenty-one-year-old kid, vomited all over his shoes. Reminder: This was at seven. The sun hadn't even set. I rolled down my window and told the two dudes with Javier that I was happy to take them home, but the guy in the vomit-covered shoes needed to make other plans. (Note: I let a puke-covered Hilton Head partyer in my car once before that night. Mistake. But I'll get back to that in a minute.)

Fortunately for Javier, one of his pals was willing to look out for him while I took the other dude home. During the ride, the friend told me their golf plans got rained out that day, and Javier had been switching between liquor and beer since noon. Apparently, no one taught him the sage advice has served so many well:

"Liquor before beer, never fear.

Beer before liquor, never sicker."

IT'S COLD IN HERE

Speaking of hangovers and vomit-covered shoes, one of my most memorable rides involved both in Hilton Head. It was a muggy summer night when I picked up a couple from Charlie's L'Etoile Verte, a fancy French restaurant on the island. When I arrived, the husband staggered to my car and plopped into the backseat. The wife followed and got into the front seat.

This was not normal. Before COVID, it wasn't unusual for a passenger to sit in the front seat, but it was rare for couples to not sit together in the back. Occasionally, a husband sat in the front and left his wife in the back, which I always thought was weird. But a woman never sat in the front, while her husband lounged in the back.

Soon as she got into the car, she glared at her husband. The chill cut through the cotton T-shirt I was wearing. Elsa had nothing on this lady's piercing glare. (If you don't have kids, that's a Frozen reference.) Fortunately, the awkward, uncomfortable ride didn't last very long. While driving, I gathered that the husband drank too much. The wife was not happy with her husband, and the hangover he had in his future would be the least of his problems.

Short as the ride was, it wasn't short enough. Midway through the ride, horrible husband started making gurgling noises and tapping on the window. I realized we weren't going to make it to the Marriott without a roadside vomit stop. Unfortunate, but only a minor inconvenience. It became more inconvenient when his drunken aim caused him to puke all over his feet. I didn't realize what happened until he was back in the car and smelled liked a guy who just vomited all over his shoes.

His scent sent his wife over the edge. Now, she wasn't just coping with anger. It was coupled with embarrassment. She apologized profusely for her "sloppy, stupid husband" and said his name—Charles—with a tone that made the hair on my neck stand up.

When we arrived at the Marriott, she bolted into the hotel before Charles got his door open. As he ambled toward the hotel, I felt a little sorry for him. His tomorrow was guaranteed to suck. Elsa the ice queen tipped me $20. It was a nice gesture that barely covered the necessary car wash and bottle of Febreze. So after all that, the ride was basically for entertainment value only.

CANCEL ME THIS

Another memorable ride from Hilton Head wasn't a ride at all. It was the most frustrating cancellation I ever experienced as a rideshare driver.

It was Memorial Day weekend, and rates were surging higher than I'd ever seen. The multiplier per ride was between five and seven, which meant I was making up to seven times the normal rate on every ride.

I dropped a passenger off in The BarMuda Triangle, and my next ride appeared on my screen. The rider was nearby, which meant less time hunting for the rider. Because of the surge, this $40 ride was able to be a $200 ride. To make things even better, the ride would take me toward Beaufort. That's a win-win-win.

The only problem? My passenger wasn't where the app said she was, and she was too drunk to provide her location. Desperate to find her and cash in on this opportunity, I called her. I tried to figure out where she was, but she and her friends were uselessly drunk.

After some fruitless, frustrating driving around, hunting and talking to her, the lady canceled the ride. Like that, my dream of a profitable drive home vanished. To make matters worse, I realized where she was after my next ride. She was only one street over. Another liquor-induced loss for the rideshare driver.

#UberProTip—Your driver doesn't have any control over the state's alcohol laws.

INTOXICATED IRISHMEN

"Here is to a long life and a merry one, a quick death and an easy one, a pretty girl and an honest one, a cold pint and another one."—Irish Proverb

Good rides lift your spirits, and good times linger long after the passengers exit the vehicle. But the same is true for bad rides. The bad juju from a combative or belligerent passenger seems to stick around all night. Many nights have been ruined by just one passenger, and some nights I shut the app down and quit early because I couldn't get back in the groove after having to deal with one too many drunken jerks that night.

One of my best and worst rides both involve a carload of Irish folks.

SEALED WITH A KISS

Let's start with the good.

I picked up a carload of older Irish passengers from a downtown bar. My task: get them home, where they have no intention of stopping the party. From the moment their Irish accents met my ears, I knew it would be a good ride. But I had no idea how much fun it would be.

We exchanged the normal, initial pleasantries. Then they began to banter just before the conversation turned to Irish drinking songs. Once they hit song mode, the rest of the ride was a wonderful karaoke concert. Their infectious enthusiasm and joy had me smiling all the way to their destination.

As they prepared to exit, I thanked them for the concert. One of the men told his wife to give me a tip. Next thing I knew, she was climbing into the front to plant a kiss on me. Since I'm a happily married man, I brushed her away to the uproarious laughter of the rest of the group.

"Honey," her husband said, "I meant this."

The man handed me a $20 bill and retrieved his wife. The group sauntered off, trailed by smells of alcohol and sounds of laughter and song.

AN EXTRA $7

Now for the negative side of the Emerald Isle.

The ride started at the same downtown bar. Two Irish dudes emerged, entered my car without incident, and gave me their destination.

It was a good, long ride—one I was happy to score. Then the trouble started, and we hadn't even made it off Bay Street.

Apparently, seat belts aren't a thing where they are from. I'm a good driver, so no big deal. Then they rolled down the windows down and started hanging out of the car.

"Hey guys," I said, "can you relax a little?"

They ignored my request. Then I spied a beer bottle in one of their hands. I stopped immediately and asked them to empty the beer and roll up the windows. They couldn't believe my requests, and all hell broke loose.

I warned them to chill out or get out, but they didn't get the message. I didn't intend to leave them on the side of the road—I'm not a monster, after all—but they continued to be belligerent. So, I returned to their pick-up spot and politely asked them to leave the vehicle. They did not respond politely.

They started screaming that they wouldn't get out of the car until I gave them their money back. This put me in a tricky situation. Remember—I don't have their money. They paid Uber, not me. After several minutes of their histrionics, I threw $7 at them and demanded that they get the hell out of my car.

They refused. Since they were stopping me from taking more rides, I called the cops. Still, they refused to leave until the officers finally arrived.

When the Irish boys finally left, they got escorted to the back of a police car. An officer took my statement, while they sweat in the patrol car. I couldn't help myself from being petty. I told the officer that I didn't want them arrested, "but," I said, "I do want my $7 back."

The officer agreed that was fair. A couple minutes later, she brought me $14. Suppose she collected seven from each drunk before releasing them to find another way home.

All in all, not a bad ride. I made $7 extra and got a great story, and they didn't go to jail. A reasonably decent ending for all.

#UberProTip—A kiss is not an acceptable tip, but twenties are!

JENNIFERS

"Toss your hair in a bun, drink a Starbucks, put on some Britney, and handle it."

Jennifer isn't really the name of these ladies, but I couldn't tell these tales using their real names. So, I'm lumping them all together as the Jennifers.

Visualize a single—but in a relationship, but it's complicated—mid-twenties to early thirties white girl. She's got a job, but she isn't quite sure it's a career.

I've driven a lot of Jennifers over the years, and I know a little bit about them. Unsurprisingly, after these rides, I've never picked up either of these ladies again.

JENNIFER #1

It's wedding season, so Saturday night is busy in Beaufort. I started out with some short rides from local hotels to the historic district, where Beaufort's few restaurants and bars are clustered. Then I began rolling down Bay Street to find the passenger that I'm supposed to pick up. It was a nice fall night, so I had my windows down.

Out of nowhere, Jennifer #1 appeared.

"You're my ride!" she insisted.

FIVE STAR RIDES

Like most in the area, Jennifer was tipsy. She tried to get in the car, so I came to a stop. Yes, she tried climbing in while I was still moving. I tried explaining that I wasn't her driver, but I failed. Inebriated Jennifer insisted she knew me, that I was her driver, and that I was taking her home.

I shook my head in disagreement as she canceled on her real ride. I told her that to be her driver, I would have to cancel my ride, too. If I did that, I wouldn't get paid.

She swore to pay me. Then, she started digging through her purse. As she digs, she shoved cash in my hand—way more than what her fare would be. I laughed and figured I had no choice. I was taking Jennifer home.

At this point, Jennifer's friend emerged. The friend yelled at Jennifer for running away and leaving her alone. Jennifer explained that I would take them both home. Pacified, the friend got in, and we hit the trail.

Unsurprising, Jennifer's friend was a Jennifer, too. A regular user of the app, I already knew she was also an awful passenger. If I knew they were together, I wouldn't have let either in the car.

The original Jennifer looked ready to pass out until something on Snapchat caught her attention. A moment later, a snap from a mutual friend provided inspiration. Jennifer decided that I needed to be in her next Snap, even though I was busy driving.

She leaned over and got the Uber-driver selfie Snap. Miraculously, I managed not to wreck and kill us all in the process. When we reached her complex's parking lot, she blurted out that she wasn't feeling well. I stopped the car and she managed to get out of the car before projectile vomiting.

Almost. The interior of my passenger door took the brunt of her first vomit spurts. Her Jennifer roommate gathered her up and walked her home, leaving me to find a place to clean Jennifer's vomit off my car door.

This is why random cash rides are dangerous. We weren't on the app, so there was no cleaning fee. So, I was stuck looking for a safe place to clean vomit in the middle of the night. Not as easy as you may think.

JENNIFER #2

The second Jennifer's story also starts on Bay Street.

Disheveled, she walked out of the bar and recognized my car instantly. I've driven her to work and home several times before. She was a decent customer who always tipped on rides to work, but never on minimum-fare rides home from the bar.

Jennifer entered the vehicle, looking perplexed. Though not quite hammered, she clearly wasn't in the greatest state of mind.

"Hey," I said, "how are you?"

"I just kissed my boyfriend's best friend," she said. "It's okay, we'll work it out. I don't really feel like talking."

With that, I spun forward and shifted the car into gear. She asked me to turn the music up. I obliged.

"Louder," she said. "You're awesome—five stars."

Her phone rang. I kept driving while she talked to her boyfriend on the phone.

"Hey," she said, "can you take me back to where we just were? I'll tip you $20. I'm not going to sit at home and wait on him all night."

I'd driven less than a mile. So, yes, I was willing to take her back.

The rest of the five-minute ride, she talked non-stop. She talked about how much she wanted to be married and have a baby. She compared her boyfriend with his best friend whom she just kissed and was going back to hang out with a bit longer.

I dropped her off and told her to have a nice night. She repeated that I was awesome and that she'd tip me on the app.

If you've read any previous stories, you know how this story ended. She didn't tip me $20. She didn't tip me at all. To be honest, if she had tipped me, I would have bet that the story wouldn't have a happy ending.

Speaking of her story, here's the rest of it. I'd driven her boyfriend before. He was a walking, talking cliché—exactly what you'd expect from a pretentious frat boy, down to the pink shorts and overuse of the word *bruh*. When Jennifer told me she kissed someone else, I didn't blame her. I was even happy for her. But kissing her boyfriend's best friend was probably a bad choice.

#UberProTip—Don't kiss your boyfriend's best friend at a bar.

KAT'S FRIENDS

"I'm grateful for my psycho, insane, and just totally messed up friends. Normal people scare the crap out of me."—Kat, probably

I have a friend, Kat. She's a people person who seems to know everyone. I've run into Kat on a number of occasions while picking up other passengers. Other times, Kat calls and asks if I can drive her and her friends home from a night out. I'm always happy to help, because driving friends at the end of the night is always better than waiting for random drunks. On top of that, Kat always tips and never does anything that would get her name in this book. The same cannot be said for some of her friends.

MEET KAT'S FRIEND

One of Kat's friends became a regular customer. She lived near downtown, and I picked her up multiple times at downtown bars or friends' houses. It didn't matter where I picked her up, she was always hammered.

On rare occasions we had interesting conversations, but usually we had the same conversations over and over at a very loud volume. She tried to be nice, but she was drunk and couldn't remember what we talked about the last time I drove her. I never really worried about her though. As long as she was talking, she wasn't throwing up.

Then on one ride, she went quiet. I tensed up. I heard her moving, so I knew she was alive. I looked in the rearview mirror and realized she'd laid down in the backseat. Next thing I knew, she dropped into the floorboard of my backseat, where she stayed until we arrived at her house.

By the time we got to her house, she was so comfortable that she wanted to stay on the floorboard. Obviously, this was a problem. I couldn't take more rides or go home to my wife with a drunk woman in the backseat. So, I begged, pleaded, and eventually convinced her that her bed, her couch, or anywhere not in my car would be a better place to sleep.

Once she agreed, I had to figure out how to get her off the floorboard and out of the car. When I finally made it happen, she made the obligatory drunken promise of an extra big tip. The "extra big tip" never came, but she likely doesn't remember a single thing about her drunken ride home.

FRIENDS IN ABUNDANCE

I once drove Kat and her friends home. All was going well. Conversation was pleasant enough, and I was making the rounds, dropping off one friend at a time. Things got unpleasant when I was left with Kat and one other lady.

Kat's friend decided she didn't want to go home yet. Loudly and drunkenly, she told me to drop Kat off at home and then take her back downtown so she could continue her night. Kat tried to convince her that this was a bad idea, but she wasn't having it.

After a lot of back and forth, I thought Kat had gotten through to her friend. When we pulled up to Kat's house, I thought the ride would have a normal conclusion. I was wrong.

The friend found out that Kat and I knew each other. She was suddenly mortified at her behavior and decided that the only way to make up for it was to excessively tip me. She started handing me cash and dropping even more into the front seat. Never one to turn down drunken overtipping, I watched with gleeful anticipation. After all, tips are one of the only perks of the job. Unfortunately, Kat was too good of a good friend. Almost as fast as the friend dropped the cash, Kat stuffed it back in her friend's purse.

Kat convinced her friend to sleep it off at her house, so I could be on my way. I didn't get the tip, but at least I got rid of Kat's drunk friend. Or so I thought.

I started pulling away as they walked toward Kat's house. Before I got out of sight, Kat's friend made a break for it and took off running. Yes, this fully grown, highly intoxicated woman broke into a full sprint, running away from Kat's house like Jackie Joyner-Kersee. Where was she going? I have no idea. They were miles from any night life. Fortunately, she ran out of gas soon. Kat corralled her and got her in the house, where she may be sleeping to this day.

That's what you get for stealing my tips, Kat!

LYFT VERSUS UBER

Even though Lyft is older than Uber, Uber has always been and always will be the market leader in ridesharing. Uber executives quickly established a renegade reputation through their cutthroat willingness to skirt regulations. Lyft saw an opportunity to grab some customers by marketing itself as the kinder, gentler rideshare company that treated passengers and customers with respect.

As a driver and passenger, I've used both platforms. Let me tell you, the kinder, gentler thing isn't true. Everything Uber is, Lyft is. Uber is just better at it in my experience.

EARNINGS: ADVANTAGE UBER

As a driver, the bottom line is earnings. In my market, it's much easier to make money on Uber than Lyft. There are several reasons for this, but generally Uber dominates the market share, which means more rides and more profitable rides are available on Uber.

LONG-DISTANCE PICKUPS: ADVANTAGE UBER

Uber started paying a premium for long-distance pickups years before Lyft. This is a big deal outside of urban markets, since you typically go farther to pick up passengers. Early on,

Uber started compensating drivers for that time. Even with both companies now paying bonuses for longer pickups, it's still better to take the rides on Uber. Why? Because Lyft compensates for the long pickup bonus by lowering the base fare for the ride.

WAIT TIME & CANCELLATION FEES: ADVANTAGE UBER

Uber pays if a customer makes you wait at pickup. After two minutes, Uber charges the passenger and pays drivers for wait time. Lyft includes wait time in the fare. As a result, you don't get paid at all if a passenger makes you wait. After seven minutes, you can mark the ride as a no-show and cancel the ride. Uber then automatically pays you a cancellation fee based on how far you had to drive to the pickup location. There are virtually no exceptions.

With Lyft, you only have to wait five minutes before you can mark the ride as a no-show and cancel. However, the cancellation fee can be as low as $2, and there's a fifty-fifty chance that Lyft will actually pay for the cancellation at all. Lyft makes all kinds of exceptions for cancellation fees. If their estimated arrival time was wrong, you don't get paid for arriving at the pickup spot too late. If the passenger put their pin somewhere you can't drive (like in a river or the second floor of an apartment complex), Lyft won't pay the cancellation fee. Their rationale? You're too far away from the pickup spot.

TRANSPARENCY: ADVANTAGE UBER

Uber shows what passengers pay for their ride. This

lets you compare that to what you made, so you can see Uber's take rate. Lyft never shows what customers pay. This is because Lyft regularly charges passengers inflated prices without passing any of that to the drivers. A sure sign that they are the more compassionate option. On the last airport ride I ever took for Lyft, they charged a couple $247 for a ride that should have been less than $75. There was no reason for a surge price, as it was a slow night—but I was the only driver available, so Lyft decided to take advantage of the couple's need to get to the airport. If not for our conversation in the car, I wouldn't have known that Lyft charged such an inflated fare and kept three-quarters of it for themselves.

RIDE & RIDER INFORMATION: ADVANTAGE UBER

Rider information is one area where Lyft should have an advantage over Uber. Unlike Uber, Lyft allows drivers to see a picture of their passengers. However, Lyft doesn't require passengers to use this feature. As a result, more than half of my passengers use a fake picture or no picture at all. So, that's a relatively useless feature. Uber also comes out on top for doing a much better job in showing rider pickup and drop-off locations. Uber uses cross streets to geolocate. Lyft just flashes a map that only gives a general idea of where passengers are and where they want to go.

SCHEDULED RIDES: ADVANTAGE UBER

Scheduled rides aren't great on either app, but they're far better on Uber. In some markets, the app allows passengers to schedule rides that drivers can accept ahead of time.

Generally, on Uber these rides aren't worth taking, but on occasion they are. The key factor is that Uber shows exactly what you'll make and what time to arrive for pickup. You accept the ride at that time and get paid the exact fare you were shown unless the rides changes.

Scheduled rides for Lyft are a cluster in every way. You accept the ride, and then Lyft shows pickup time and estimated fare range. This is where the problems begin. Let's say you accept a 1:00 p.m. pickup for a ride with an estimated fare of $8–10. At 12:30 p.m., regardless of how far from the pickup point you are, Lyft pings you for the ride and sends you to the location. When you arrive ten minutes later, Lyft informs you that you're early. Then you have to wait until 1:05 p.m. before you can cancel the ride for any reason. If you don't head straight to the pickup because you stop to get gas or use the restroom, you're in trouble. Since you arrived later than Lyft's ETA, you're no longer eligible for a cancellation fee. Yes, if you arrive at a pickup twenty minutes early but Lyft wants you there twenty-five minutes early (and you get paid zero for this wait time), they refuse to pay a cancellation fee if the rider doesn't show. Rider no-shows are a huge problem on Lyft scheduled rides, because they're often medical rides scheduled by insurance companies. These medical trips don't get modified if appointment times change or passengers find other transportation. Even if the passenger shows up, you are still getting screwed because ninety percent of the time, Lyft doesn't honor the estimated fare they show you. Your $8–$10 fare turns into a $5 ride even after you wait at the pickup point for twenty-five minutes. Essentially, you can spend forty-five minutes driving and waiting to make

$5. And abandon all hope of a tip. Third-party rides never include a tip of any type.

CUSTOMER SUPPORT: ADVANTAGE UBER

Uber support is awful. It is maddeningly frustrating. Wait times to access a real person drag on for eternity. If you're willing to jump through enough hoops to get connected to a person, that doesn't guarantee a happy ending. Assistance often ends due to an Uber policy or a language barrier, so you wait forever and end up disappointed. With in-app messaging, you'll likely get connected to multiple people on the same issue. Get traded to another rep and expect different answers and explanations to the same question. High-tier drivers are supposed to receive better support, so if you want better support, jump through more hoops on a daily basis.

That said, Uber support is so superior to Lyft support that there is no comparison.

There is no way to call Lyft. All communication takes place through a dysfunctional in-app chat system. They take hours to respond, and if you don't reply immediately to their delinquent response, they close the chat, forcing you to start over again. Even if you reach someone, ninety-nine percent of the time you get canned responses with little connection to your question.

Uber support staff also appear to have occasional flexibility to fix problems and make things right for drivers. Lyft never does. Uber consistently paid cleaning fees and damage claims when passengers made messes in my car. In all my time driving for Lyft, they never honored a single claim I made. Because of this, I stopped taking Lyft rides at night. I couldn't risk a vomit incident if Lyft wouldn't pay to clean my car. One hundred percent of the time, Lyft takes passenger's word over the driver's word. More than once, Lyft took back the fare from a completed ride because the passenger claimed the ride didn't happen. In five times as many rides with Uber, Uber has only done this once.

While Lyft is almost impossible to contact when you need something, they bombard drivers with communication when they want to change driver behavior. In response to legal issues and PR snafus, Uber is closer to treating drivers as actual independent contractors without any pretense of punishing drivers for acceptance rates and cancellations. Lyft hasn't. Lyft sends repeated emails and pop-up messages, chiding drivers for not accepting or canceling rides. If the messages don't work, they log you out of your account. Still don't respond to their annoying behavior-modification attempts? Lyft will send you a poor passenger experience message and suspend your account for as long as an hour. Lyft has temporarily suspended my account multiple times after I canceled rides that would have required me to drive unaccompanied minors or children without car seats. While annoying, it had little impact on my behavior. I just shrugged and flipped open the Uber app.

These are a few reasons I've taken 500 percent more rides with Uber. Uber treats drivers better, pays them better, is more transparent, and is easier to deal with. Don't get me wrong—I'm not saying Uber never exploits drivers or customers. But in a side-by-side comparison, I would choose Uber every time.

FIVE STAR RIDES

#UberProTip—Rideshare companies spend millions developing a plan to encourage you to use their apps the way they want you to. As a passenger or driver, you get exploited if you don't plan how you want to use the apps.

MASSHOLES, MARINE WIVES & THE MURDAUGHS

"God is good. Beer is cold. People are crazy."—Billy Currington

Because most rides are uneventful, I quickly forget names, faces, and details. Some rides have so many layers I might not believe it if I wasn't there myself.

This ride started out normal enough. I pulled up to Skull Creek Boathouse, a waterfront restaurant on the north end of Hilton Head Island and quickly found my passenger. As happens so often, she told me that we needed to wait for two more people. Minor inconvenience, but it could be worse. As we waited, we started in on small talk.

Madison explained that she was visiting from Boston. I casually asked her what she was down for. She looked at me with a sparkle in her eye and a strange, school-girl giddiness.

"Anything!" she said. "What can you get us?"

I felt a little lost and rephrased my question: "What did you travel down south for?"

"Oh, a wedding," she said, "but what kind of drugs can you get us?"

She obviously misunderstood my initial question. I tried to convince her that I don't have any idea where to get drugs, but she won't let it go. Just then, her husband and friend arrived, which shifted the conversation.

Madison and her husband, Owen, took the backseat, and the friend sat up front with me. I immediately sensed that something was wrong. Apparently, we left the friend's husband at the restaurant after a marital spat escalated into something more extreme than an everyday argument.

A few minutes into the ride, Madison and Owen burst into drunken karaoke, singing their lungs out to the radio. While they clearly felt no pain, their front-seat friend alternated between tears and anger texting. Eventually, the texting turned into a phone call, the phone call became a yelling match, and the yelling devolved into threats about what the girl's dad and brothers would do to her husband when they learned what he did to her.

All the while, the backseat passengers were oblivious to their crying, screaming friend.

"Turn it up—I love this song!" Madison called, eager to up the ante on Dance Party USA.

After a few minutes, the couple asked me to stop so Owen could grab something for their final destination. I obliged, and Owen jumped out of the car. While he was gone, the two women talked about the upcoming wedding.

"You can't go to the wedding without a date," the backseat drunken karaoker insisted. "Our driver should go with you."

The last thing I wanted was to get in the middle of a

domestic dispute and hang out with these people, so I flashed my wedding ring.

"I'm not sure how my wife would feel about that," I said with a laugh.

Fortunately, that killed that conversation, but it reminded Madison that I hadn't helped them buy drugs. She again begged and pleaded and insisted for me to hook them up with something—"even just a little weed." Once again, I told her I couldn't help with that.

The husband returned, and we headed to our destination without any more drama. As Madison exited the car, she paused and smiled.

"Bet you don't get many rides like that do you?"

Before I answered, she said, "Don't mind us—we're just Massholes."

SURGING IN SAVANNAH

I don't really like driving in Savannah, but there's money there. Many profitable nights occurred when a passenger in Beaufort or Hilton Head took me to Savannah and I drove there until the end of the night. In fact, the most profitable ride I ever took on the app came from Savannah. As you could guess, it wasn't just a ride. It was a whole thing.

It all started around 8 p.m. on a Friday when Uber sent me a long-ride notification. I accepted because it would take me to Savannah, Hilton Head, or Charleston. In any of those places, I would make way more money than if I was stuck in Beaufort all night.

I arrived at Andrea's apartment, and she and three friends soon emerged. It was girls' night out, and they were dressed to kill in fancy clothes and done-up hair. As it turned out, they were all Marine wives. Not surprising. The Beaufort area is home to the Marine Corps Recruiting Depot–Parris Island and a Marine Corps Air Station. In some circles, the word Marine can carry baggage. There are many negative assumptions and stereotypes, but the Marines I encounter don't fit that mold. The typical Beaufort Marine and wife are quite different. They are some of my favorite people— the exact opposite of the violent, abusive, hard-drinking stereotypes that some people perpetuate. The same is true for Marine wives. I have also yet to meet a Marine wife who is an uneducated, trashy ex-stripper.

However, Andrea and her friends are why stereotypes exist. They feared they would have a hard time getting home at the end of the night. They bought into the unfounded hysteria that Uber drivers were part of a criminal network that raped and killed unsuspecting passengers. Thankfully, I didn't strike them as the rape-and-kill type, so they asked if I would stay in Savannah all night and drive them home when they were done partying. This ensured I would get paid for the hour-long ride home, but it came with risk. If these party wives flaked on me, I'd be stuck in Savannah late at night and have to drive home with no passenger.

I rolled the dice, and we exchanged numbers. Then I told them to call me when they were ready to go home.

It was a typical Savannah night. I did well driving, and the surge rates made even short rides worth taking. However, Savannah nights are long. Last call is at 3 a.m.—an hour later than South Carolina.

Around 2 a.m., the girls called me to pick them up. I got

to their location and loaded them into the car without much trouble. Though the girls asked me to drive them home, they wanted to use the app for the ride, despite that making the ride more expensive for them. I was fine with it. Surge pricing was in full effect, and the ride home would cost them nearly four times as much as the ride to Savannah.

As the ride started, they were in a good mood. It was a turn-up-the-music-and-roll-down-the-windows ride. All was well until I made a fatal mistake.

They asked to stop so they could grab some pizza at a nearby spot. I was still a new driver. I didn't know how bad this could go, and I didn't want to risk losing the ride home, so I agreed. It didn't take long for them to grab their pizza. In a few minutes, they were back in the car.

At this point, I could tell it had been quite a night for the girls. If you've ever heard the song "Tequila makes her clothes fall off," you have an idea of what I'm talking about. Over the course of the night, the fancy outfits and done-up hair were replaced with the drunken stripper look.

They ran on adrenaline for the first half of the ride, loudly and lewdly describing their night of dancing. Despite being sloshed, they curated their pics, careful to ensure each was safe to post, excluding access to people they didn't want seeing the pictures. But the adrenaline only lasted so long. By the time we approached Andrea's apartment they were all knocked out.

Thanks to my rides with Andrea and the girls, I made more than $500 that night. Nights like that keep drivers putting up with the crap Uber drivers take with each shift. How else could a non-profit employee make $60 an hour?

Speaking of the crap drivers put up with, I quickly learned that no matter how late I finished driving, I had to do a visual inspection of my car's interior and exterior at the end of the night. You never know what a passenger might leave. (Keep reading for that story!) That night's find wasn't the most interesting, but Andrea's friends had eyes bigger than their stomachs. After all the hassle to stop for pizza, they left a box of uneaten slices and a couple of half-eaten pieces on the seats. I had to clean the car to lose the pizza pieces and smells, but it was a small price to pay for a $150 drive home.

INFAMOUS

Recently, there's been a lot of talk with passengers about the drama surrounding disgraced lawyer Alex Murdaugh and his family. Because Hampton is so close to Beaufort and some key events in the sad drama have taken place here, Beaufort and the Murdaughs are linked in the mind of many tourists. Between media coverage of the trial, podcasts, and the Netflix documentary, everyone wants to know something about the Murdaughs. Whether I'm picking up passengers in Beaufort, Hilton Head, Savannah, or Charleston, the topic comes up every week on at least one ride.

While I don't believe I have ever driven a Murdaugh anywhere, it's within the realm of possibilities that one of them was one of my late-night passengers during the Beaufort Water Festival. Luther's, the downtown Beaufort bar where Paul Murdaugh stopped before crashing his boat into a bridge and killing Mallory Beach, is a frequent late-night pickup point. A recent passenger visiting Beaufort asked me to make a stop at Luther's on her way to dinner. She wanted to run inside and see it in person after watching the Netflix documentary.

NAVIGATION ISN'T AS EASY AS YOU THINK

"Roads? Where we're going, we don't need roads."—
Emmett Brown, PhD

You would expect a multibillion-dollar, global technology company that's capable of tracking riders and drivers all over the world and immediately matching the closest rider and driver to have a handle on directing drivers from pickup to destination. AI that crunches data to create the perfect, profit-maximizing price should be able to direct drivers to a location that hasn't changed in fifty years.

You would expect that, right? Wrong.

One of the hardest things rideshare drivers deal with is navigation through the Uber and Lyft apps.

START TO FINISH PROBLEMS

The trouble often starts before you pick up a passenger. The app claims that your passenger is one place, but your passenger isn't there. Sometimes, it's user error, sometimes a drunk passenger just wanders off, but often it is an issue with the app. Regardless, it's difficult to make a pickup when the passenger location and pickup point provided by the app aren't the same place. In addition to wasting time, this makes the ride more awkward or uncomfortable since it starts with a pissed-off passenger.

Other times, the location is correct, but the app recommends a route that won't get you to where you need to go. This requires you have to backtrack and discover how to access the pickup spot on your own. Remember—you get paid for none of this wasted time. You can't even start your wait-time timer until you reach the app's designated pickup point, which—again—might not be where your passenger is.

Compounding the issue is that many passengers struggle to use the app correctly when sober, so they have absolutely no shot while in their highly intoxicated condition. I can't tell you how many passengers drop pins in the Intercoastal Waterway and then get mad when I can't find them. It seems an easy fix, as no passenger thus far has actually wanted me to pick them up in the ocean. Unfortunately, about eighty percent don't reply to messages asking to confirm their location. My favorite response is when I ask a passenger to confirm their location and I get this reply: "I'm here." Super helpful! Clearly since I'm not getting paid to look for you, if I knew where here is, I would be there, too.

Another frustrating version of this conversation occurs when passengers repeatedly ask where I am instead of stating where they are. This usually happens when someone requests a ride from a specific location that's different than their actual locale. I go exactly where I'm told to go, but the passenger won't tell me where to find them. In a residential neighborhood, being off by a house or two is an easy fix. In crowded downtown areas, there is no easy fix.

Once a passenger gets in the car, the navigation issues continue. The app may send you the quickest, easiest route—or, it might not. If the app's navigation causes the trip to take extra time and cover more miles, they don't adjust your fare.

Equally frustrating, the app might tell you to turn just after you pass the street. Other times it completely skips turns. You may need to make a right on to MLK and then a left on West Bay, but all you see is a left on West Bay. Sometimes the app tells you to turn onto roads that don't exist or to make turns that put you driving the wrong way down a one-way street. The app will even have you drive in a circle to start the route from your original point.

And the excitement doesn't end at your location. When you arrive at your destination, the app may tell you before or after you get there. If the passenger or driver knows the directions, these are minor inconveniences. With a new or poorly marked destination for both, it's very difficult to know where to go.

Another navigational "glitch" causes more than half of all passengers to be two or three minutes further away from you than the app states. I see Kat's eight minutes away and needs a ride. Once I accept the ride, Kat is magically whisked eleven minutes away.

You might not think this is a big deal, but it means more time driving that you're not being compensated for. Two or three extra minutes on each ride over the course of twenty rides means an extra hour of unpaid driving.

A new, even more curious "glitch" in navigation began occurring frequently on the Lyft app after they introduced upfront pricing to keep pace with Uber. Since Lyft now shows drivers a passenger's destination and fee, I often accept rides that show upfront information only to find out that the actual ride is fifteen or thirty minutes longer than the upfront information promised. Making this even more sus is the fact that this "glitch" only occurs on long rides—those rides that Lyft has difficulty convincing drivers to accept because the pay isn't worth the time.

#UberProTip—For best service, when requesting a ride, make sure you are where the app says you are and answer your driver's questions.

ONLY THE BEST

The inspiration for this book came from reader reactions to #UberProTips I posted on social media. After driving on Friday nights, I would post an edited version of my experiences on my timeline. Most people thought the posts were hilarious and wanted more. Dozens of people responded to the posts, insisting that I should write a book about my experiences. The more I thought about it, it was a good idea. Not everyone agreed though.

Apparently, my stories rubbed some people the wrong way. (Or perhaps they hit too close to home.) At one point, I received negative feedback for commentating on entitled and intoxicated folks I drove. Another time, an acquaintance had read enough stories about bad passengers. Exasperated, she asked me if anything good ever happened while driving.

In truth, the answer is no—there aren't many good things that happen while driving. Most rides aren't awful or fantastic. They're neutral. This is fine with me, and I consider those uneventful rides to be "good" rides. I pick up a passenger at point A, nothing much happens, drop off the passenger at point B, and get paid.

Sometimes, rides suck for reasons outside of the passenger's control—bad directions, bad traffic, or bad luck.

With bad rides, something ruins the ride that is directly

related to the passenger's attitude, action, talk, or smell.

Only a very few rides are considered "great rides."

What makes a ride great?

1) **Profit.** The ride is much more profitable than it should be. The bottom line is that I drive for a rideshare company to make money. When surge pricing or customer tips turn a $10 ride into a $30 ride, it's a great ride.

2) **Fun people.** Some passengers love life. If they invite me into their joy, that can be a great ride. These are the turn-your-music-up-and-sing-along passengers, the we-are-having-a-good-time-tonight-and-so-are-you people. A ride like this can give the boost I need to drive for another couple of hours.

3) **Good conversation.** On occasion, I drive some truly interesting people. They have cool stories or intriguing life experiences that they share. Or we share a mutual connection or a common interest, and we pass the whole ride in an enjoyable conversation.

4) **Regulars.** Picking up people I know and enjoy driving are always great, especially if they turn into regular off-the-app customers. It's always a relief when a passenger name or address pops up and I know they're good people. This beats picking up random strangers anytime. It's even better when they start calling me to drive them without using Uber as a middleman. (Rideshare drivers, don't try this at home without state approval, commercial auto insurance, and an LLC to avoid legal issues.)

BEST OF THE BEST

Who are the best customers I've had in my years as a

rideshare driver? Thanks for asking. As per the rest of the book, all names and details have been adjusted to protect passenger privacy—even if I'm saying nice things about them.

GLENN

This bartender once asked about off-the-book rides. She wanted someone consistent, since it was so hard to get a late-night in our town. I agreed to do it, and she was thrilled. She also said that her boyfriend worked nights and might like a ride from time to time. I said it was cool to give him my number, too. That turned out to be a great decision.

I drove her to and from work occasionally, but I drove the boyfriend (Glenn) all over the place. In fact, he may be my all-time best customer—an interesting dude everyone who knew and had great stories. I never told him the price for a ride. He always paid more than I would have asked. When a text came through from him, he moved to the front of the line.

Eventually they didn't need me to drive them anymore, but we are still friends and Glenn is still my favorite customer of all time.

ROBIN

Another bartender. They're my favorite passengers, as we bond over dealing with drunks and relying on tips to make our jobs worth the effort. Robin moved to Beaufort after COVID-19 and realized that finding an Uber was difficult. I told her I would be happy to pick her up anytime, and she took me up on it. I regularly took her to work. She returned the favor by always paying more than I asked and sending other passengers my way. Cool people like Robin who overtip or overpay are my kind of customers. When they regularly send riders my way, they move up even further.

CHEYENNE

Another food-and-beverage worker, Cheyenne hitched rides from me all the time over the years. She was funny and had me laughing every ride. Even though I picked her up as she moved from house to house and job to job, she always insisted on going through the app. That was fine with me. She always tipped, and those tips got bigger and bigger over the years.

By the time she left town, Cheyenne tipped at least $10 a ride. She did this while working two jobs to make ends meet. Her excessive tipping wasn't the only reason I questioned her judgment. A previous DUI left her with a suspended license, and she had a wake of useless boyfriends. But we were cool, and our conversations were always interesting.

ALEXIS

Another regular, she always paid through the app and almost exclusively got rides to and from work. Rides with Alexis started in the good/neutral category. She was quiet and unentertaining. But when she started requesting Uber XLs and leaving $5 tips, she became one of the greats.

Toward the end of my time driving her, she complained about how hard it was to find rides during the week when I was out of town. I explained that her ride was short, and drivers could see how little they would get paid, so they declined. I explained how I could tell a ride was for her before I accepted it, and since she was polite and a good tipper, I always accepted. She was surprised that most locals didn't tip and tipped me $10 that day.

The next time I picked her up, I thanked her for her $10 tip. When that ride ended, she doubled the tip. I was shocked. This single, retail-working mom dropped at least $30 to get to work! And the pattern continued for a month. She requested an XL and tipped $5, $10, or $15 every ride. She never wanted to schedule directly and never said anything other than "You're welcome" when I thanked her for large tips.

Eventually, she settled back into $5 tips. Then one day, without a word, the tips stopped. After years of tipping on every ride and a six-week barrage of extraordinary tips, the tip well dried up without any explanation. I gave her a few more rides, but after a few more weeks, I never saw her again.

GRAHAM

He was a regular dude who liked his happy hour. Don't think I ever drove him more than five miles at once, but I drove him a lot. Occasionally, I drove him and his wife for date night, but most often it was a short trip to the neighborhood bar for happy hour. He was the perfect customer. He always checked with me before hitting the app, was always polite and on time, and he always paid cash. The only bad thing I can say about Graham is that he was friends with Bob, the star of the chapter "Ditches and Dents."

WILSON

Much like Graham, Wilson became a favorite because he was easy to deal with and paid well. The hardest part was getting to Wilson inside his gated community with temperamental gates. The ride was always the same: pick him up for dinner at the nicest restaurant in town, then pick him up a couple of hours after a couple drinks at the local dive bar.

Every time, he'd ask how much the ride was, then pay me double for both rides. Always cash, always easy. If more passengers were like Wilson, this would be quite the gig.

HILTON HEAD ISLAND BAR CRAWL GIRLS

I don't remember their names, but driving them around was memorable for all the right reasons. They collectively invited me into their joy and treated me like a human being, not an automaton that got them from point A to point B. I picked them up late in the afternoon before their bar crawl. Since they didn't want to worry about getting the wrong Uber driver later that night, they offered for me to be their driver for the night. They seemed fun and harmless, so I accepted.

Like many at Hilton Head, they were living their best life and having a great time on their beach vacation. They'd clearly downed a few beach beers in preparation for their night out, but they were tipsy, not trashed. The Island is small enough that I commonly pick up the same passengers at the beginning and end of the night—even through the app. The transformation many passengers go through from the beginning to the end of the night is always unmistakable, sometimes hilarious, and other times depressing. Outfits go from exquisitely put together to crumpled and disheveled. Earrings, phones, and purses get lost. Conversation volume goes way up or down.

With the Hilton Head girls, the transformation came in stages. I repeatedly ran into them at pickups and drop-offs, even while they weren't riding with me. Fortunately, they stayed as friendly and chill while drunk as when I first picked them up.

As often happens, the bar crawl turned out to be all they could take for the night. When I picked them up, they begged me to stop at a gas station and Pizza Hut so they could finish the night in their condo with White Claw and pizza. They paid enough for two stops. Besides, they bought me a drink and gave me a couple of slices, making it worthwhile to break my self-imposed policy against stopping to meet passengers' whims.

AMIR

Sometimes memorable passengers are sober. Amir was one of them.

Initially, I didn't want to take his ride. He was going a long way in the wrong direction late at night, so I declined. But seems it was a slow night in Beaufort, and I was the only driver available. Soon enough, he popped up on my phone, over and over. I watched Uber's algorithm do its thing and transformed Amir's request from an Uber X to Uber Comfort to UberXL.

Once he reached the XL stage, the ride was worth taking despite the long distance. Besides, he clearly needed a ride. If I didn't take him, local taxi companies would gouge him.

Generally, Uber conversations are short, superficial, or one-sided. Passengers usually have very little interest me talking after a brief interchange at the beginning of the trip. Like a bartender or psychologist, we get paid to listen, not talk. But when I picked up Amir, he flipped the script. Fantastically grateful and engaging, Amir gave me one of the best Uber-based conversations of all time.

While I drove, I learned that we were in similar places in life and wanted the same things for our families. We discussed our children, family vacations, concerts, the places we'd traveled, and the places we wanted to go.

Sixty-five quick minutes later, we reached Amir's destination. He said he would tip on the app, and when my phone confirmed that his tip came through, I wasn't surprised. He was just that kind of guy.

PIRATES, POLICE OFFICERS & THE PURSUIT OF PROFIT

"Who's been drinking tonight? Everyone but me, officer."

It might be hard to believe, but the time I called the cops to remove drunk Irish passengers from my car wasn't the only time I ran across the blue lights while driving for Uber. It wasn't even the only time I called the cops to get a passenger out of my car. The other situation isn't much a story, but I was concerned about my safety.

CRAZY, AND NOT THE GOOD KIND

It was a late weekday night, and I was picking up my last ride of the night. There were no issues at pickup or on the way to his destination—Burger King. But when we reached the BK, the guy's crazy came out.

He told me Burger King was just a stop. He asked—well, demanded, really, that I wait as he went into Burger King. He explained that when he returned, I was to take him to Hilton Head.

I explained that he didn't put that in the app, and I wasn't taking him that far. He was, after all, my last ride of the night.

As you could guess, he wasn't having it. He then alternated between begging and demanding that I wait as he got his food before taking him where he wanted to go. I reminded him how rideshares worked, but he showed no signs of understanding. Instead, he launched into a psychotic episode.

He mumbled and talked to himself, then alternated arguing with me and the voices in his head. Not wanting to waste more of my night, I told him the ride was over and asked him to exit the vehicle. He again refused. After more unsuccessful attempts to get the guy out of my car, I dialed 911.

Thankfully, the officers arrived quickly. Though he initially refused to get out for them, the cops eventually got him out of my car so I could end my night.

My interactions with the police as a rideshare driver have been overwhelmingly positive. The police realize that rideshare drivers keep drunk drivers off the road.

Despite this, it's never a good feeling when blue lights are flashing at a pickup point. It's a sure sign that there won't be a seamless, quick pick up. Even more worrisome is when an officer approaches my car instead of a passenger. That's what I encountered one Saturday night in a residential neighborhood near the Isle of Palms.

MEETING CAPTAIN MORGAN

The officer explained that my passenger was coming out

the house. All sorts of questions ran through my head when the officer commanded me to take the passenger to the address on the app without any stops or change of destination. The uniformed officer wouldn't share any details, but I gathered that this was a domestic issue.

While the introduction rattled me, the ride was quiet and anti-climactic. What got it on these pages was the passenger's outfit. When the guy emerged from his house, he was dressed from head to toe as a pirate. He wore a hat, eye patch, hook, and a real wooden peg leg. He even had the fine details down, smelling and sounding like he recently bathed in a bottle of rum.

I held back on all my best pirate jokes, and we took the short ride to his hotel in awkward silence. Once there, he staggered out, and that was it.

Thus concluded the only ride I've ever given to a pirate.

GOOD EVENING, OFFICER

As a rideshare driver, I have to monitor what people bring into the car. Drinks are never a good idea, because most passengers assume South Carolina's open-container laws don't apply to Uber passengers. Spoiler alert: They do.

Besides the illegality of it, open liquor containers are bad for business. They spill and leave wet seats, stains, and smells. Most people understand and toss or chug their drink. However, some people manage to sneak something past me when they enter all three doors at the same time.

This happened as I transported college kids from Bay Street to a cheap hotel during Water Festival. As we pulled up to their hotel, cops were everywhere. It was only then that I realized one of the not-so-sober girls had a glass bottle of beer. I tried to find a new drop off point, but it was too late. One of the officers spotted the beer. He signaled for me to stop and asked them to exit the vehicle. Fortunately, all he wanted was for the beer to get poured out and the bottle thrown away. He didn't even make me stop to explain what happened.

An equally entertaining police interaction occurred during another ride from Bay Street.

It was a good late-night ride. All four passengers were having a great night. They were well lubricated and saw no reason for the ride home to stifle their joy.

As we made our way through Port Royal, I eased off the gas pedal. In this ticket-hungry town, the police force has a deserved reputation for being difficult to deal with. I never take my chances there. (Unrelated side note: While living in Port Royal, we had several negative interactions with law enforcement. 1. My wife got pulled over for not signaling a right turn from a stop sign. 2. The police got called to my nine-year-old daughter's birthday party by a grumpy neighbor. 3. I got pulled over for an alleged hit-and-run on my own vehicle. This one was possibly called in by the same grumpy old neighbor.)

While driving through Port Royal, a car followed a little too closely, and his lights made it difficult for me to see. Normally, I would have sped away from the jerk, but I was in Port Royal. And the one rule there: You don't speed in Port Royal. So, I did the opposite. I slowed down, hoping that would encourage the guy to pass me and get his lights out of my eyes. It didn't work. The annoying driver tailed me up, across, and down the bridge going over Battery Creek near Parris Island.

Shortly after, we crossed the bridge. Before I exited Port Royal, blue lights filled my rearview mirror. Confused, I pulled over to the side of the road and I rolled down my window. An officer walked toward me with the swagger of a man who just made his community safer by getting a drunk driver off the road. When he reached me, he twitched as if the smell of beer pouring out of my car nearly overpowered him.

He tugged at his breeches with pride, certain he was about to make a DUI arrest. He asked if I knew why he pulled me over, and I said I had no idea—especially since I wasn't speeding. The officer informed me that my right rear wheel crossed the fog line as we crossed the bridge, and that mistake was a moving violation.

"Sorry," I said. "I was having a hard time seeing. Someone was on my tail, and their lights were impacting my ability to see the road."

He grunted and crossed his arms. "Who's been drinking tonight?" he asked.

To this, my carful of passengers gleefully shouted that they had all been drinking. I corrected them, stating that everyone but me had been drinking heavily.

"That's why I'm their Uber driver," I said, pointing to my clearly visible Uber sign and open Uber App.

His excitement at busting a drunk driver subsided as he realized his fishing expedition had gone awry. "Make sure you drive safely," he said tersely and walked away.

BLUE LIGHTS IN THE REAR VIEW

Driving so much makes me very aware of how poorly people drive. Not using turn signals, driving under the speed limit in the left lane, or driving as if participating in a NASCAR race are expected parts of the daily experience. Driving late at night makes me aware of how many people drive who should call for a car instead. Watching people weave in and out of their lanes, unable to maintain a consistent speed keeps me on my toes. This leads to my last and most harrowing experience with blue lights.

I was making my way home from Hilton Head late at night when a car flew past. I was cruising at nearly 70, and he must have been moving at 100 miles per hour or more. Shortly after he blazed by, blue lights approached at a similar speed. I slowed down as multiple officers passed by in pursuit of the speeder.

A few minutes later, blue lights raced toward me. It took a minute to make sense of the scene, because the blue lights weren't directly behind the other car. They were on the wrong side of the median-split highway. When I processed the situation, my heart raced, and my body tensed.

The speeding car was not on the other side of the highway. It was driving toward me—on the wrong side of the divided highway! I jerked the car into the right lane, barely avoiding the speeding, wrong-way driver.

I pulled over for a couple of minutes to process what had just happened. Then I reentered the roadway and headed toward home. My hands trembled, but I survived. Slowly, my breathing and heart rate returned to normal. I relaxed my grip on the steering wheel. Then, it happened again!

The speeding car bore down on me from behind, even more blue lights chasing him. As the cars and blue lights disappeared on the Broad River Bridge, I decided to take the long way home, hoping it would get me out of this mess for good.

I turned right onto Savannah Highway and made the remainder of my journey home uneventfully. That was the most thankful I've ever been to get home safely.

I don't know what the driver did, but he didn't want to get caught. Escaping the cops is best left to the movies though. Whatever he did initially, leading police on that kind of chase only made things worse for him. I never found out what was going on, but I heard the chase made it into Beaufort before the speeding driver was finally apprehended.

#UberProTip—Don't make your driver call the police to get you out of the car. And if you're in South Carolina, open container laws apply to you, too.

QUIET ONES

"That's why crazy people are so dangerous. You think they are nice until they are chaining you up in the garage."

Quiet nighttime passengers make me nervous. The later it gets, the more nervous I get with them. Are they going to pass out? Are they going to throw up? Are they planning a robbery at the place we're stopping? Are they working out the details of a drug deal? Are they plotting to murder me and steal my car?

You may think these questions are the product of an overactive imagination, but every scenario happened to me or a fellow rideshare driver. On the other hand, similar stories have emerged in which rideshare drivers or people pretending to be rideshare drivers have been the perpetrators of crimes. As a result, passenger safety has become a huge topic of conversation. It really ramped up in my home state of South Carolina after the murder of a University of South Carolina student, who drunkenly got into the wrong car. She thought the guy was her Uber driver. He wasn't.

To date, fifty-five rideshare drivers have been murdered while working. Statistically, passengers and drivers are as likely to commit crimes against or otherwise harm one another. That's why many drivers—including nearly every driver in an urban environment—records every second of every ride with a dash cam. It's also why I refuse to pick up people who use an obviously fake name. Try getting picked up as Daddy, Bad Baby, or Redfox, and I'll cancel your ride every time.

PASSENGER PASSED OUT?

One of my first St. Patrick's Day rides in Savannah was a dude who staggered into Broughton Street traffic. Soon as he saw my Uber sticker, he flagged me down. Drunk as he was, he unfortunately managed to correctly identify me as his assigned Uber.

At the time, I was green enough to think I had to pick up every passenger, even if they were dangerously intoxicated. I reluctantly let him in the car, fervently praying that my St. Patrick's Day wouldn't get cut short by early evening, alcohol-induced vomiting. The real money wouldn't pop for a couple more hours. I didn't want it ruined by a random dude's inability to hold his green beer.

The fear factor was increased by the length of his ride. I had to get him from the historic district to a nondescript neighborhood on Wilmington Island. Could we do it? I had no choice but to find out.

Other than my internal anxiety, the ride was uneventful all the way to his driveway. When I pulled the car to a stop, he didn't move. This wasn't the first time a passenger nodded off in a drunken stupor, so I didn't think much of it at first. I got to work.

I turned on the lights, cranked the radio, and yelled that

we had arrived. Nothing. I tried again and got an incoherent grunt in response. Having reached the limit of my patience and anxious to return to downtown's surge pricing, I broke out the driver's magic words.

"I can call the police or an ambulance—your choice."

This inspired some erratic movement. Eventually, he figured out how to make his hands move to the seat belt and door handle. Then he convinced his feet to carry him out of the car. No part of the process was fast or smooth. Staggering toward his house, he used my car to steady himself. That's when a brilliant idea hit him. He didn't have to walk the extra ten feet to his house and look like a moron trying to shove the key in the lock. He could look like a moron right here. So, he did.

He dragged himself onto the tailgate of his pickup truck, flopped into the truck bed, and settled in for the night.

PASSENGER GOING TO THROW UP?

Oh yeah. Several passengers have puked over the years, but that's not for this chapter. We'll get there, though. And when we do, those stories are exactly what you expect. They're gross. They're sad. They're disgusting. They're infuriating. And once they're in the rearview mirror, they're funny.

PLANNING A ROBBERY AT THEIR STOP?

Fortunately, this didn't happen to me. It did happen to a fellow driver, when a man in Michigan got arrested for using his Uber as a getaway car after a bank robbery. Why didn't he use his own car? His driver's license was suspended.

A few minutes after dropping the bandit off, the poor

driver got a surprise. Multiple police cars pulled him over, and officers surrounded his car with guns drawn. They screamed for the driver to exit the car, which he did. I can't imagine what he was thinking at this point, but I'm certain that there is no way the money that driver made on the ride was worth the trauma of getting pulled over at gunpoint.

GETTING CARJACKED, SEXUALLY ASSAULTED, OR MURDERED?

Again, none of these have happened to me, but it happens to drivers—often. A quick Google search brings up articles highlighting the events in Baltimore, Chicago, Houston, Charlotte, Chattanooga, Pittsburg, and Detroit. And that's just the first page. Click to page two, and the results go on and on and on.

One recent story from Florida revealed that police found the dismembered body of an Uber driver in the trash outside a gang member's apartment. Even for non-rideshare drivers, that kind of story should send shivers down your spine.

This hit home recently when the Beaufort City Police announced the arrest of a woman I'd given multiple rides to. Her crime? Homicide. She shot her boyfriend in the head in their apartment.

WORKING OUT DETAILS OF A DRUG DEAL?

This has absolutely happened to me, but I didn't realize it at the time. Because I drive in a small town, I drive some people regularly. Some of them schedule rides directly with me, and then I drive them even more regularly. This is how

I learned I was driving a drug dealer as he worked out the logistics of his drug operation.

I picked up the dealer at his stash house. (Note: I didn't realize this was his stash house. I thought it was simply his house.) I can't remember where I took him, but that's not relevant. Thankfully, he didn't come back to the car with a backpack full of product.

While driving him around town, he had the strangest phone conversation about Molly and cowboys, candy and footballs, yellow jackets and snowballs and cookies. It wasn't a memorable ride, but it was odd enough that I mentioned it to a regular I picked up next.

She was a nice girl and an above-average tipper. Despite this, she'd spent some time around drug users, which endowed her with an extensive drug-centric vocabulary. She laughed as I recounted the conversation, then explained that the guy was using me to run him around while taking or placing drug orders.

I felt naive, but it's confirmation that you learn something every day as a rideshare driver!

I forgot about the exchange until a few weeks later. While scanning the local news, I found a story about a drug raid in Beaufort. Any guess where it took place? You got it.

My passenger's stash house got raided, and my passenger—the alleged mid-level drug trafficker—sold drugs to an informant. Who knows? He may have made the deal that got him busted in the back of my Honda Civic.

#UberProTip—Your Uber driver is just as scared of you as you are of him!

RIDICULOUS RIDER BEHAVIOR

"Rum is the reason pirates never ruled the world."—
Toby Keith

You can break down rideshare passengers into two categories: sober and . . . not sober. While there is some variance between passengers, the clear dividing line is whether or not the passenger or passengers are sober. If not, the next line measures just how drunk passengers are.

I've struggled to understand what would cause someone to behave the way certain passengers do. They say horrible things and make ridiculous demands. They treat others like trash. They take career-ruining photos. While I suspect some horrible behavior is due to the anonymity that ridesharing affords, I suspect a more tangible culprit. When you boil it down, rum is the most common reason.

Some folks can handle their liquor. Others can't. Some people are wise enough to drink in moderation. Others lack such self-control. Alcohol turns people into energetic, funny friends or belligerent, belittling jerks. It brings out their best qualities or makes them angry and abusive.

My general policy is that if passengers want luxury, private car service treatment, they should make arrangements with a luxury, private car service or offer to pay me to accommodate their extra requests. When they order the cheapest UberX ride available, they should expect to get from point A to point B safely and quickly, but they aren't entitled to anything they aren't willing to pay for. This rubs some passengers the wrong way. And that's okay, because ninety percent of my low ratings come from drunk or mean passengers I wouldn't want to drive again anyway. That's the upside of the rating system. If a passenger or driver gives someone three or fewer stars, the system unpairs them. The algorithm pays attention and won't match the two again. When a horrible passenger gives me a low rating, it's a win for me. It guarantees I won't ever have to drive them again!

BEYOND THE BOOZE

Setting aside awful drunken behavior, the biggest issues drivers face from passengers are wait time and stops. Corralling a group of revelers is never easy. Add several hours of drinking to the mix, and it turns routine late-night pickups into slow, obstacle-laden events.

For me, several factors go into whether I'll suffer the full seven-minute wait time or cut my losses and move on. If some passengers arrive on time and are waiting for their friends, what are they like—friendly and apologetic or drunk and disinterested? What time is it? Where am I? How busy is the night? How long is the ride? Sometimes, it's a busy night, and I can't afford to wait. As soon as I cancel, I get another ride in the same general location, making waiting a poor financial decision. Other times, the cancellation fee pays more than the ride. When that happens, I lose money by taking the ride. So . . . canceled.

Want to see a Karen get pissed? Tell her the wait time has elapsed and you're canceling the ride. Watching her climb out of the car to order another ride because her friends won't come out of the bar is a sight to see. There's always cursing and anger. Get lucky and you'll get a slammed car door. Sometimes, Karen's anger isn't directed at her driver. Sometimes, she's pissed at her friends. Whoever gets her wrath, I guarantee her face will be as red as her hair.

Stops are the other issue. Passengers typically don't understand that drivers are independent contractors, not employees. Uber may allow riders to request something, but the driver isn't obliged to do it every time.

As a general rule of thumb, I decline every ride that includes a stop. They aren't worth it. Wait time fees are a joke, and that waiting makes every ride less profitable. Since many drivers feel this way, passengers have resorted to creative ways to trick drivers into taking their rides.

They may request a ride without stops. Then, just before you arrive, they add an extra stop or two or three. They think you're stuck as their personal valet. I don't play that game. When passengers attempt this stunt, I immediately cancel the ride or inform them that I don't do stops as they enter the car. I then politely explain that I can either drop them off at their stop or their original destination. This gives them options. They can offer to pay me fairly to make the stop, be dropped off at either location, or cancel the ride and hope to find a driver desperate enough to accept a ride with stops.

This conversation goes several ways depending on the type of passenger. Most understand math, see your point of view, and agree to one of your options with no fuss. But there are others who are either stupid or entitled. None of these folks can grasp the concepts you try relaying to them. Stupid people respond, "I've already paid you my money. You gotta take me wherever I wanna go." Entitled folks get angry. No matter what comes out of their mouths, the translation is the same: "How dare you, an Uber driver, not acquiesce to my demands, no matter how ridiculous they are."

Passengers also attempt to work around driver choice by making changes to their destination after drivers accept a ride. If a passenger can't find a driver willing to take them several hours away, they will enter a much closer destination. Once a driver accepts the ride and is coming to pick them up, the passenger flips the switch and changes the destination.

Or they do the opposite. They request cheap, short rides that no driver will accept. Then they change their destination to a more expensive point until someone accepts. Once a driver takes the bait, the passenger changes the destination back to the closer location.

In both cases, they expect the driver to accept their changes. After all, if the driver declines the trip, they won't get paid. Even worse, they wasted their time driving to the pickup location.

When a passenger makes changes to any ride after I accept it, I immediately contact the passenger through the app. I want to know what the changes are. Because—believe it or not—drivers can't see changes after a ride is accepted. All we see is the change in fare. That's a red flag that the ride is no longer worth taking. If the passenger won't answer me or if they take any of the actions above, I immediately cancel.

THE DEADLY DUO

Of course, no discussion of rider behavior is complete without a quick mention of the two worst passengers. Typically, I see these passengers a mile away. When I do, I am quick to decline the ride request or cancel the ride immediately when the wait timer hits zero.

DRUNK DIVAS

A gaggle of women stagger out of an upscale restaurant six minutes and fifty-nine seconds after I arrive. Then they ask me to wait for their two friends who are in the restroom. After five more minutes, they emerge. This is when you find out they have three different drop-off locations. Though they paid for meals, an Uber, and the mortgage with their ex-husbands' money, they're too impatient to wait for four different Ubers to pick them up.

Because I drive in a small town, occasionally I know at least one of the women in the group. But in their condition, they often don't recognize me. Eventually, one of them will realize you know them and the people they've been gossiping about. When a passenger comes to this realization, she's always super nice the rest of the ride. Of course, that niceness doesn't often translate to a good tip.

It's also guaranteed that my vehicle will be a disappointment. It's never big enough or clean enough for the divas. They complain about how hard it is to enter or exit, and the temperature is always too hot or too cold. Following one drunk-diva ride, the last two women I dropped off spent ten precious minutes discussing how much they disliked my car.

MILLIONAIRE MISERS

A well-dressed, distinguished, older couple emerges from the antebellum bed and breakfast to dine at the most expensive restaurant in town. They easily drop a couple Gs on their weekend getaway, but they won't walk a quarter mile to their restaurant. They also won't tip on their minimum-fare Uber ride.

They wait twenty minutes for me to drive across town to pick them up, even though they could walk to the restaurant and back in less time. As I pull up, I realize I'm about to get a complaint about my car. It always happens. They drop $7.62 for a five-minute ride and find something to complain about. These folks just can't help it.

Before the advent of upfront pricing, this was the worst kind of ride. It tied me up for half an hour, and I netted less than $3. Thankfully, I can now see the ride details ahead of accepting a trip, so I can look for better rides. Only the newest or most desperate drivers accept those crap rides.

Equally frustrating are the well-to-do riders who are determined to pay as little as possible for a ride. They pinch every penny they have, and they have a lot of them. These dudes arrive in town on a private plane for a golf trip. A single round of golf costs more than a rideshare lift to the resort, but they insist on piling their whole foursome and clubs in an UberX to save a couple bucks.

Several years into my driving experience, I upgraded from

my Honda Civic to an SUV. This allowed me to take rides as an UberX or at the higher levels of service, Uber Comfort and UberXL. As an unexpected consequence, passengers started trying to get UberXL service at UberX prices. My vehicle is big enough to handle more people, so I get it. But it's wrong. When this happens, I politely explain that they didn't pay for the ride they want. So, they can either cancel their ride and reorder an UberXL or pay me the difference directly.

This conversation is usually quick and painless, but not with the millionaire misers. They demand I drive out of the parking area and onto the airport runway to load their bags and clubs into my vehicle. I remind them they didn't order the correct service level, but it's usually useless.

On this occasion, my loaded passengers were adamant that they were being reasonable, and I was a jerk for not doing what they wanted. I raised my phone and showed them how it worked on the app. One passenger wanted to work it out, but his buddy had different plans. He swigged his Bud Light and called me an asshole for a second time. Normally I would have just laughed and driven away, but this time was different. I knew no one would want to take them where they wanted to go. So, I sucked it up and tried to help them out. Mistake.

When I said I'd help them out, but not at a discounted rate, the ringleader suggested we take the ride off the app.

"We'll just pay for you to take us to the course," he said. "Fair enough?"

Now we are getting somewhere, I thought. I was wrong. The guy then proceeded to offer me half of what Uber would charge them for the ride—$3 less than what Uber would pay me for taking the ride as an UberX. When I declined, his buddy threw down his Bud Light and let loose a volley of expletives.

I wished them luck and left them at the airport with their golf clubs, suitcases, and cheap beer.

#UberProTip—Don't be condescending and rude to someone trying to help you, especially if you don't have a backup plan.

SURGE PRICING

"Do your job. Get paid. Go home."

In the rideshare world, 99.9% of drivers drive for one reason. They want to get paid. They either want or need extra money or they desperately need to pay their bills. There's no other reason why a person would subject themselves to dealing with rideshare companies, drunk passengers, and vehicle wear and tear. Under normal circumstances, the money is okay. When Surge pricing kicks in, more money comes faster.

The mechanics of surge pricing are supposed to be simple. When driver supply drops or passenger demand rises, dynamic pricing kicks in and prices increase in that geographic area. Surge is good for the rideshare companies and for drivers. Everyone makes more money with surge. And passengers also benefit, since they don't have to wait long for a ride. They just have to pay the premium price.

Surge pricing mechanics have undergone multiple changes as rideshare companies discovered how to package dynamic pricing to be more palatable for customers and more profitable for the companies. Initially, surge pricing relied on a simple multiplier. When in place, surge pricing increased fares to one and a half, four, or nine times the normal price—whatever the algorithm decided would bring balance to supply and demand. This caused problems though. Because while sober people can be bad at math, drunk people are consistently worse. Much worse. Since the total fare didn't show up until the end of the ride, many passengers woke from their drunken stupors to rides that were way more expensive than they expected.

Angry passengers shouted their disappointment, and the rideshare companies listened. App developers got to work. Soon, riders could see the total cost of any given ride. Passengers even had to confirm they understood what the ride would cost when requesting it.

Known as upfront fares, these fees get calculated based on the multiplier times the base rates for any given area. These base rates come from an area's rate card.

What's the rate card? It was a tool that Uber and Lyft originally used (and still claim to use when it benefits them) to tell passengers what they would pay and drivers what they would get paid.

The rate card included information including:
- **Base Fare**—The amount they charge you for getting in a rideshare car.
- **Price Per Mile**—What each mile of a trip will cost. This gets added to the base fare.
- **Price Per Minute.** What each minute of a trip will cost. This gets added to the base fare.
- **Minimum Fare**—The lowest fare possible.
- **Wait-Time Fee**—The cost to make a driver wait. This gets added to the fare.

- **Cancellation Fee**—What passengers get charged if their ride gets canceled.
- **Local Tolls, Taxes, and Surcharges**—Additional fees that are out of Uber and Lyft's hands.

Drivers have a similar card that lays out income potential for the same categories. The rate cards vary from market to market and change constantly. As you would guess, the changes rarely benefit passengers or drivers, although rideshare companies worked hard to convince you that the changes were made for your good and not their bottom line.

Prior to the COVID-19 pandemic, a driver typically took home 50–70% of a ride's fare. This is no longer the case, as once upfront pricing debuted, the companies no longer had to link fares to the rate card.

A few years ago, the surge multiplier phased out for drivers and passengers. However, dynamic pricing stuck around, so prices still go up when things get busy. But since passengers now agree to or reject upfront fares, rideshare companies no longer show a multiplier or a rate card. They just charge whatever they think you'll pay without telling you how far above the normal rate you're getting charged.

Eliminating the multiplier set rideshare companies free. Now, the algorithm does its thing with no encumbrance. It generates prices based on data about you, people like you, your zip code, your pickup address and destination, and the type of ride you request. The goal: Charge the highest possible price you'll accept for every single ride. Reject a high price, and the algorithm prices you more accurately next time. Agree to the fare, and your charge may increase slightly on the next ride, just to see how much you're willing to pay.

Despite these changes, losing surge wouldn't work for drivers. Too many drivers rely on surge pricing to make driving worthwhile. Knowing this, rideshare company execs had to find a solution. They needed to convince drivers they were getting surge pricing while increasing their own profit from every passenger's fare. The solution? Surges became flat fees instead of a percentage of passenger charges.

In driver land, the map changed from 2.0x, 3.0x, or 6.0x to $5, $7, or $15 surges. This might benefit drivers on short rides, but more importantly, it allowed rideshare companies to pocket more cash on surge rides.

Example:

Multiplier Surge

Passenger base fare is $15.

Driver takes 70% of base fee, which is $10.50.

With a 3.0 surge, the base fare becomes $45.

Driver take with a 3.0 surge becomes $31.50.

Rideshare company's cut with the 3.0 surge is $13.50.

Flat Surge of $10 (instead of 2.0, 3.0, etc.)

Dynamic pricing pushes passenger base fare from $15 to $45.

Driver take with a $10 surge is $20.50 ($11 less than previous).

Rideshare company's cut with the flat surge is $24.50 ($11 more than previous).

As you see, even with an unusually high $10 surge, rideshare companies increased their profit by nearly 100%. All it took was cutting driver pay.

I'll talk more on this in a future chapter. For now, it's enough to know that rideshare companies are shifting from burning through venture capitalist funding to turning a profit. Their biggest obstacle to profitability is how much they pay their non-employee drivers. Since every dollar they don't pay drivers increases their profits, they're continually seeking ways to increase their take rate. Many of these techniques are borderline illegal, and some are downright exploitative.

#UberProTip—Always tip your driver, especially on short rides. If the ride costs you less than $15, a $5 tip will likely double what the driver makes. If your ride seems expensive, the rideshare companies are making more, not your driver. On surge rides, your driver probably takes home less than half of whatever you get charged.

TYBEE TO SAVANNAH: FROM BACHELORETTES TO BACCHANAL

"Ask me if I want another shot, I'm practicing saying, 'I do.'"—Random Bachelorette

Tybee Island is a barrier island about ten miles outside of Savannah, Georgia. Its proximity to Savannah and alcohol-friendly beach has transformed the once-quiet coastal beach town into a party spot. If you want to see how wild things get on Tybee, search Twitter for "Orange Crush Tybee." Just don't do it at work or around children.

The island is also a popular spot for bachelorette parties. Groups of giddy young ladies rent a house and spend all day on the beach that's an Uber ride away from the nightlife of downtown Savannah. Anytime I drove in the Savannah area, I would pick up at least one carload of giggling bachelorettes powered by a White Claw buzz, heading to or from Tybee. These rides were always loud and inevitably required me to wait the full seven minutes for the last straggler to make it out of the house or the bar.

I never minded the rides though. They offered guaranteed entertainment. And once the passengers sobered up the next day and contemplated their actions during the ride, they tipped well.

The psychology of bachelorette rides is also intriguing. Of all the bachelorette passengers I've driven, they fit into four categories.

PASSENGER 1: DRUNK AND DONE

She's ready for bed—right now. She stumbles to the car and will try to get in the wrong car at least once. If not for passenger three, she would have never made it home.

PASSENGER 2: DRUNKER, LOUDER, AND NOT READY TO GO HOME

She brings a ridiculous list of embarrassing things the bachelorette must complete during the night. She wants one more shot, then a final one. She then makes everyone wait while passenger three drags her out of the bar to stop her from hooking up with a stranger.

PASSENGER 3: THE ENFORCER

She's the most sober passenger, and she ordered the Uber. She asks my name and checks my license plate before letting the drunker ones crawl into my car. She spends all night alternating between shots, water, and shooing away dudes hitting on the bride-to-be.

PASSENGER 4: THE BACHELORETTE

This character has the most variance. Sometimes she resembles passenger one—she went hard and is out for the count. Sometimes she's more like passenger two, making sure she has one last epic night before married life. Sometimes she's closer to passenger three and is absolutely mortified about what her drunk friends are doing and saying on the ride back to Tybee.

Bachelorette parties from Tybee to Savannah or vice versa were always good rides. The long drives always came at peak times and usually included surge pricing. It was also a welcome escape from the downtown area. I drove nights in Savannah occasionally for the money, but I always hated it.

Late-night driving in Savannah is stressful. The nightlife scene is popping, which means crowded streets and difficult, confusing pickups and drop-offs. Tight roads, traffic, and highly intoxicated passengers means waiting and never knowing what kind of person would climb in the car.

Of all the places I've driven, Savannah draws the highest percentage of people who intend to get dangerously drunk every night of their visit. City officials seem to be okay with that, as they allow folks in the entertainment district to walk from bar to bar alcohol in hand.

Being aware of pedestrians is critical. While crosswalks get daytime use from sober people, drunken late-night revelers meander all over Savannah's dark streets. This describes most weekends in Savannah, but it isn't sufficient for St. Patrick's Day weekend.

BEWARE ST. PATRICK'S DAY

For some reason, St. Patrick's Day is taken very seriously in Savannah. Traffic issues and rider behavior become off-the-charts awful. Hence why the money is so good for rideshare drivers on that weekend. The first year I drove in the midst of the chaos, I made $400 after midnight. But after going at it for three years, the money wasn't enough to bring me back a fourth time. The traffic and risks from out-of-control, dangerously drunk passengers made St. Patrick's Savannah a no-go zone for me.

The last straw came when it took twenty-six minutes to drive just over half a mile. When I got to the pickup site, I learned that my passengers were a pair of teenagers who got absolutely smashed with a fake ID. One look made it clear that they were high school students. Yet somehow they found a bar to serve them. Thanks to that bartender's bad choice, I was stuck with the dilemma of whether or not to drive drunk, unaccompanied minors or trade their triple-digit fare for a $4.02 cancellation fee.

MOVE . . . GET OUT THE WAY (LUDACRIS)

In all my years of driving, I've only been involved in one traffic incident. It was a doozy.

The road from Savannah to Tybee is well traveled, especially in the summer and on holiday weekends. As you drive, the road changes from four lanes to two and back again, requiring a good deal of merging. The ever-shifting lanes also cause traffic to stall if everyone decides to head to or from the island at the same time.

One Labor Day weekend, I ended up on Tybee and

caught a ride back into Savannah around dinnertime. I wasn't the only one leaving the island. The road was filled with people headed into Savannah after a day at the beach.

Traffic was stop-and-go at times but moved well most of the time. In my rearview mirror, I noticed a red sedan weaving in and out of traffic like a clown. Clearly the dude didn't play well with others, but not a real concern. He was behind enough cars that I never considered I would have to deal with him. However, I underestimated how badly he wanted to make it back to Savannah.

The weaver made up the gap between us with alarming speed. Unfortunately, he didn't make it before the lane merged from four to two lanes. So, he was stuck behind me until the highway expanded back to four lanes. More unfortunate, he wasn't going to let anything stop him from his destination, even physical obstacles.

Instead of respecting the laws of physics, he continued driving until he rear-ended me. He didn't hit me at full speed, but he wasn't crawling. Like any normal person, I pulled over to the side of the road to deal with the accident. Like a psycho, he floored it, passing me and the line of cars in the turn lane and speeding off to Savannah.

As I processed what happened, I realized the guy was an evil genius. He hit me so I would pull over and give him turning lane access to pass everyone else. He moved so fast I couldn't get a plate number, but someone else did and called in the accident.

Since my vehicle wasn't seriously damaged, I took my passengers to dinner before spending the rest of my night dealing with police and the insurance company. It took a couple of days, but Chatham County Police located the driver and charged him with a hit-and-run.

He must have found a place to stash the car and sober up, because when I Googled him, I found a long history of substance abuse and poor driving. On the bright side, he was insured at the time. My insurance company filed a claim with his insurer, and my car got repaired in a couple of days at no cost to me.

It was a minor inconvenience, but it gave me more empathy for full-time drivers who would have been without income while the car got repaired. This incident also showed me how bad the Uber's driver insurance is. I would have been on the hook for $1,000 or more if the other driver wasn't located and I had to file a claim with Uber's insurance carrier.

UPFRONT PRICING IS JUST ANOTHER WAY TO RIP YOU OFF

"Google did it by being better, not by being Al Capone. 'Don't be evil' ring a bell?"—Bill Gurley

In a previous chapter, I shared how upfront pricing allows rideshare companies to uncouple prices from the rate card. By making this change, they can charge passengers however much the algorithm determines they'll pay. Upfront pricing exploits drivers in the same way.

By giving drivers an upfront fare, executives use the algorithm to generate the lowest fare each driver will accept. It's a simple formula

Highest price for each individual passenger for every ride

+ Lowest price for each individual driver on every ride

=

Maximum profit for rideshare companies

Pay attention to news stories about rideshare companies and you know they insist drivers are independent contractors—not employees. You also know the companies get accused of mistreating and exploiting drivers. They've even been sued for their business practices in several states.

I recently came across an article about an Uber driver who got carjacked in Atlanta. The article stated that the driver's car sustained thousands of dollars of damage, and his smartphone and other personal items were stolen. Uber offered $1,000 to cover his insurance deductible. But there was a kicker—they would only pay if the driver signed a non-disclosure agreement that prevented him from suing Uber, disparaging the company, or sharing the details of his carjacking and settlement.

The general, truthful consensus is that the rideshare business model is predicated on the companies oscillating between treating drivers as employees and independent contractors, based on which perspective is advantageous to the company's bottom line at any given moment. The lawsuits and barrage of bad press resulting from this bipolar approach have substantial effect. Rideshare companies spend a lot of time and money changing their platforms and trumpeting how these changes benefit drivers and riders alike.

Despite the best efforts of their public relations staff, the stories they tell are almost never true. A change that is positive for drivers inevitably comes with a Trojan horse. Drivers get excited only to learn that the execs already have another change in the pipeline that will put more cash in their pockets and drivers back at square one.

The best example of this was when they rolled out upfront pricing for drivers.

Since their inception, Uber and Lyft have given drivers as little information about their potential rides as possible.

A pin flashes on a map with a small, hard-to-read passenger rating and distance to the pickup. Drivers then have a few seconds to decide whether to accept the ride. Keep in mind that not accepting most rides prevents you from accessing premium driver rewards.

Because of this, I accepted many rides early on without knowing who I was picking up, where the passenger was, where they were going, or how much I would get paid. Sometimes I didn't even know if I would get paid for traveling a long distance to pick up the passenger. Instead, the screen flashed that "This ride may qualify for a long pickup fee." Taking the ride was a risk. Even when I accepted, I only got the passenger's name and pickup location. I didn't know whether the ride was five minutes or five hours long until the ride started.

Obviously, drivers hated this. They'd take rides, spend twenty minutes driving, and make a measly $3.

Eventually, however, the drumbeat of negative media and threat of legislation forced rideshare companies to deploy upfront pricing to drivers. Doing so actually fit their narrative. It was the type of change that their lawyers could credibly say proved drivers are indeed independent contractors.

After this change, drivers began receiving all necessary information to accept or decline rides wisely. They still only have a couple of seconds to make the decision, but a quick informed decision is a step in the right direction. With the advent of upfront pricing, drivers also see a more precise passenger location, which includes the mileage and time to reach the passenger. Drivers receive the same information about the rider's destination and learn exactly how much they'll get paid for completing the trip.

I was ecstatic when this change was introduced. Just before it was released, I was on the verge of quitting. But when they gave me the information I needed to screen rides, I could focus on rides that made financial sense and leave the rest. I was back in business!

For a brief period, upfront pricing functioned as promised. As a result, I began to decline far more rides than I accepted. While my acceptance rate plummeted, I made more money in less time each week because I skipped the rides that were bad for my bottom line.

Great as it was, it was short-lived. Within a few months of upfront pricing arriving in my market, the rideshare companies unleashed its hidden plans, and the platforms became even more exploitative of drivers. Here's how the exploitation broke down.

1) Drivers were no longer linked to a rate card. Because drivers accepted rides based on an upfront price, the rate card no longer applied. What Uber or Lyft offered as payment was sometimes exactly what the rate card would have paid. More often than not, the payment decreased. Also, if their estimated times or distances weren't correct, the error was the driver's problem. Drivers didn't receive compensation for longer drives or additional time. They did it all for free. Occasionally, a fare got adjusted if "support" deemed it appropriate. But that was rare. And there was no rhyme or reason to their decision making. Most times, drivers got a cut-and-pasted message stating that upfront pricing is better for drivers, while their policies prove the opposite.

2) They began manipulating fares to make surge rides less profitable for drivers. Because my market is so small and I decline so many rides, the same ride requests often pop up over and over. I decline rides when the fare is too low for the time and distance required. Sometimes a ride appears over and over with the same fare, but often the fare increases. Sometimes a ride increases in value so much that I accept it half an hour after it first appeared. Other times, a surge shows up and promises drivers extra cash on the next ride. Upfront pricing has screwed that up also. Many rides I decline get offered again during a surge at an even lower price. It's a way to excite drivers while canceling out the benefit of the surge for a driver. Below is a common scenario.

Ride A: 7 minutes and 3 miles to pick up

9 minutes and 4 miles to drop off

Upfront price payment to driver: $6

Ride A with $5 surge: 7 minutes and 3 miles to pick up

9 minutes and 4 miles to drop off

Upfront price to driver: $8

Previously, such a surge offer would pile $5 onto the driver's take. Now, Uber has effectively cut the $5 surge in half by offering $3 instead of $6 for the non-surge portion of the ride. This is not a one-off glitch. It happens on virtually every surge ride. Uber counts on drivers accepting base fares they normally wouldn't accept by presenting the ride as a surge ride.

3) Uber began hiding passenger fares from drivers. For a long time, Uber outdid Lyft with transparency regarding trip costs. At the end of each ride, I could click a few buttons and see what a passenger paid and how the fare was calculated

and divided. I could even check the math to make sure I got paid correctly. Shortly after upfront pricing was introduced, the fares disappeared. Theoretically, I can log into my Uber account and access my weekly pay statement and the individual transactions and check them, but that takes much longer, and I can't do it in real time on my phone. Why would Uber want to stop showing passenger fares?

4) Uber cut rates again—dramatically. Like all other tricks, they rolled it out as a net positive. While mileage rates were cut by as much as fifty percent, pay for time spent on each ride increased a similar amount. Uber's pitch was that this change would increase driver pay for short rides significantly, while reducing pay for longer trip only slightly. This was complete nonsense. Even rookie drivers know that the bulk of a driver's earnings comes from mileage. This change made long rides almost impossible to take and improved the fare for short rides an insignificant amount. Driver fares for rides to the Savannah/Hilton Head Airport (SAV) dropped from $40 or $60 dollars a trip to as little as $23. Rides to Charleston fell even more dramatically, from $60 to $70 to $35 to $45.

Airport rides had once been the best rides a driver could hope for. With the cuts, UberX airport rides became rides only taken by inexperienced or desperate drivers. These changes might make sense if they were part of a strategy to make fares cheaper for customers, but that wasn't the case. Uber didn't cut rates for passengers at all. They charged the same amount while paying drivers less. Once again, the company found a way to increase the spread between passenger price and driver pay in an attempt to turn a profit.

VOMIT AND OTHER WAYS TO TRASH A CAR

"Your friend going to make it home okay? Because if they vomit in my car, you are getting charged a $200 cleaning fee, and the ride is over on the spot."

As a driver, one of the worst things that can happen is for a passenger to vomit inside my car. Vomit stinks, is disgusting, is hard or expensive to clean, and keeps me from making more money, because puke means my night is over. Additionally, there aren't many places to clean vomit out of a car in the middle of the night.

Fortunately, Uber and Lyft both charge passengers a $150–$250 cleaning fee if they vomit in a driver's car. However, this isn't the great deterrent you might expect. Almost inevitably, the vomiter isn't paying for the Uber. A friend is.

While a number of previous stories feature vomiting folks, only one blew chunks in my car.

MEET THE PUKERS

The first lady who vomited on a ride was a nice Marine wife. She'd been out with friends and went a little too hard on the wine. While she got sick multiple times on the ride home, she always warned me. Every time, I stopped to let her get out and take care of her business. Everything was fine until she puked on her purse. The rest of the ride didn't smell great, but we made it to her house on Parris Island. When I casually mentioned that I knew her neighbors, she slipped me a $20 and made me promise not to tell them about her ride!

The guy who made the biggest mess tried to be slick but made it worse on himself. After his initial yack, he should have told me to stop. Instead, he rolled down the window to vomit out of the car. Bad plan—really bad plan. All he accomplished was getting vomit on the inside and outside of the car doors and in the window opening. Since cleaning puke out of a window opening ain't easy, his kind friend got hit with the full $250 cleaning fee. I've always wondered how that conversation went in the Air Station barracks that next day. "How the hell did your Uber ride home cost me $262.89?" I suspect that conversation wasn't fun for either of them.

Then there was the New Year's Eve ride. After taking enough rides, I developed a sense of self-preservation. As if I had Spidey-senses, I grew to know when to cancel a ride before it starts and just take the L on that ride and move on the to the next one. Sometimes it's easy to cancel. Example: A guy can't stand up on his own to make it to the car or is angry or combative that I won't let four people ride in the backseat of my Honda Civic. At other times, it's not that easy, but the vibe isn't right, so I cut my losses and go. This was one of those rides. I knew I shouldn't have let them in the car, but I did. Then I paid for it.

It was New Year's Eve. Two girls staggered out of Luther's and said I was their ride. As soon as they get in, one girl starts to gag.

"No, not going to do this," I said. "If she is going to be sick, I can't take y'all."

Gagger says she'll be fine, and her friend backs her. Less than twenty seconds later—we hadn't even made it off of Bay Street—gagging girl vomits. Most of it gets in a bag they brought with them for that very purpose. Since I have a strict you-vomit-in-my-car-the-ride-is-over policy, I pulled over. I explained that the ride was over and they needed to find another ride home. The non-vomiting friend went apoplectic.

She ranted that she paid me, that I had to take them no matter what, and that she would give me a one-star review and get me fired from Uber. Oh, if I had a dollar for every time someone made such threats! I suspect I wouldn't need to drive anymore. At the least, it would get me a nice bottle of bourbon.

(Side story: Despite many people threatening to get me fired, I'm still taking rides to this day. The only time I talked to Uber about a passenger complaint was when a lady in Columbia got mad because I wouldn't sit in the Cookout drive-through with her. When she started ranting, I smiled and informed her that I didn't work for Uber. I was an independent contractor and could cancel rides at any time.

She really lost it when I told her the ride was so short Uber wouldn't count it as a ride. So, she couldn't even give me that one-star review she promised. She decided that reporting me to Uber for driving while drunk was a good way to get even.)

My last run in with a vomiter wasn't awful, but I feared it would be. I arrived at the pickup point and no one was waiting. After a couple of minutes, I noticed a group of people across the street. They were huddled around a woman who was in obvious distress. She was unsteady on her feet, maintaining the pose that one strikes when preparing to vomit and hoping to avoid getting any on their boots. I realized she was probably my ride, and I didn't really want it. I contemplated canceling and driving away but decided to wait it out. I wanted to see if the group would make me wait long enough to ensure I got paid a cancellation fee.

As my seven-minute timer nearly finished, one of them approached my car. To my dismay, I knew the guy. He explained the situation and asked me to take his friends home. Now I couldn't cancel the ride—at least not without being a jerk.

The husband and wife entered the car holding a big gulp cup. The husband claimed the cup would serve as a vomit cup if his wife got sick again. I rolled my eyes and told them I would happily stop if the cup isn't big enough or her aim failed.

"Just, please," I said, "please make sure she doesn't throw up on or in the car."

We made it home with only one vomit stop. They also gave a big tip when they realized I knew the guy who talked me into not canceling the ride.

SURF, SAND, AND EWWW

Vomit isn't the only liquid passengers use to mess up a driver's cars. Driving in coastal areas, one thing I deal with are people who leave my seats wet. It's understandable. They spend all day at the beach or boating. There's no way they'll be completely dry for the ride home. I try to understand. Things happen. Most of the time, it's no big deal. Throw a towel down under you. A simple explanation and acknowledgment is enough for me.

Most normal human beings know they're wet, tell me, apologize, and offer a tip. After all, they know they're leaving a mess for me to deal with. Not everyone rolls that way though. I can't tell you how many times I've had to stop to dry off my seats after passengers left them soaked without even a word.

The nice things is that one of the rideshare companies takes this pretty seriously. When I have to stop and photograph wet seats, the company usually compensates me.

Sand brings similar problems. With up to twenty strangers piling into my car in a single day, there will be bits of the stuff in my car. But occasionally, they leave my whole backseat and floorboard covered in mud, dirt, or sand.

On one particularly disgusting occasion, my seat was wet after a ride. While expected in some situations, the passenger hadn't been in or near any water. I'll let you use your imagination to guess the cause of that mess.

When a passenger leaves a mess, I have to stop and clean it immediately. Otherwise, the next passenger will complain about my dirty car. Driving a dirty car is a surefire way to rack up low ratings, and no one tips a driver in a dirty car.

FIVE STAR RIDES

Though rideshare companies don't take normal messes seriously, they occasionally reimburse me if I have to stop driving to clean my car. To get reimbursed, I have to send in pictures. If they feel the pictures are bad enough, I get some money from them for my time and frustration. But I never know whether I'll get reimbursed.

Some passengers have trashed my car. When submitted for reimbursement, Uber Support claimed it was normal wear and tear and gave me nothing. At other times, I've turned in a much smaller mess and received a cleaning fee much larger than I deserved.

#UberProTip—Don't vomit or leave any other bodily fluid or trash in your Uber.

WEED

"I know you don't smoke weed, I know this; but I'm going to get you high today, cause it's Friday; you ain't got no job . . . and you ain't got sh!t to do."—Smokey

I never knew how much I would learn about marijuana as a rideshare driver. As a former high school teacher, I knew people liked to smoke weed, but I underestimated how many Uber passengers would have just finished smoking up, be carrying, or be on their way to buy or sell weed.

Within a couple months, I noticed a trend. Virtually anyone I took to work at a fast-food joint or restaurant kitchen smelled like they just hit a fat blunt. At times, the smell was masked by other odors. At others, the smell was overpowering.

My observation led to action. When possible, I would preemptively crack a window, but weather and other conditions often forced me to keep the window up. As soon as some rides ended, I rolled down all four windows to avoid ending up high as a kite.

DRIVING THE DEAL

Another thing I never considered was the possibility of

providing transportation for drug transactions. Once Uber made it possible to add a stop to your ride, I often gave round-trip rides to shaggy-looking bros leaving their suburban subdivision for a quick stop by their "buddy's house."

The passenger always left the car holding their bookbag nonchalantly. When they came back to the car, they clutched that thing like it suddenly contained America's nuclear launch codes.

I went through this process for a fast-food employee on his lunch break. Judging from the smell when he returned, he couldn't wait out the rest of his shift to take a couple bong rips while he was in his—er . . . friend's house.

This is one of many reasons I started declining trips with stops. But some passengers weren't so surreptitious.

KIDNAP PROTECTION AGENCY

I was transporting some girls who were vacationing in Hilton Head. They were super concerned about getting kidnapped, so they hired me as their personal driver for the night. They were nice enough, and driving the same passengers is always preferred to a never-ending string of randoms, so I agreed.

The night was mostly uneventful. I took them to dinner and then to The BarMuda Triangle, a cluster of bars so close that patrons walk from one to the other all night long. At the end of the night, my fearful passengers called me to pick them up. This is when things went off the rails.

When I arrived to pick them up, the quiet nervous girls were basic white-girls, hammered. They were no longer quiet. They were no longer feeling fear. They were unable to feel pain. And they had no worries in the world. One was slightly less intoxicated than the other, so she used her borderline sobriety to corral her friend and guide her to my car.

Once the really drunk one made it in the backseat, she decided to sit in the front seat. So, she started climbing over the seat. As you would expect from a drunk party girl, her efforts were not graceful. However, she made it to the front, and we started across the island to their hotel.

On the way, they did their best to keep the party going. They wanted the windows down and the music up. I obliged and listened as they sang the whole way home. When I stopped to pay the toll, the toll attendant was not impressed with their singing. Rather, her persistent stone face didn't crack a smile.

When we arrived at the Best Western, the party still wasn't over for the girls. They planned to down some marijuana edibles and hit the pool.

In the fog of their excitement, they realized they didn't have any money for a tip. (This was before Uber enabled the tip feature on the app.) Since they felt obliged to tip, one reached into her purse and offered me a couple edibles. I declined the offer and sent them off on their swim.

LOST AND FOUND

My most serious run-in with the weed world came later though.

People leave all kinds of crap in Ubers. I've found phones, sunglasses, lighters, chargers, dog toys, and leftovers. And one night, I found a small bag of weed. (Again, I am not making this stuff up.)

FIVE STAR RIDES

While cleaning the back of my car at the end of the night, I noticed a baggie of weed in my backseat. Making matters worse, I'm not sure who left it. Obviously, the baggie came from one of my last customers. Otherwise, someone would have taken it or said something to me about it. But it's still a mystery.

My last two customers were a mom and her toddlers and a teenager working at a fast-food joint. One of them was not a happy camper when they realized what they lost. Unsurprisingly, no one filed a lost item report with Uber on it.

#Uberprotip—Don't leave belongings in your Uber, especially if your belongings are controlled substances.

X-RATED RIDES

"Well, that escalated quickly."—Ron Burgundy

Alll kinds of people do all kinds of things in their Ubers. Just when driving gets boring, a passenger does something I couldn't expect or make up. Even with all the disgusting, inappropriate things that have happened in my backseat, none included any X-rated activities. Granted, a few couples cut off their conversations, and it was clear what was happening in the backseat, but nothing ever got out of hand.

That isn't to say that rides never had adult content. You've already read about the dude who left his black card with a stripper. The next chapter tells the story of two men, a pregnant wife and another wild ride from the strip club. For now, I'm going to tell you about the time I picked up a car of passengers from the Beaufort Water Festival.

TO THE MONTAGE

They were headed back to the Montage, a luxury inn inside a 20,000-acre gated community on the May River. It's frequented by Justin Bieber, Chris Pratt, and other celebrities and well-heeled guests who want to play hard and relax harder. I don't think my passengers were famous, but all they did during their ride was talk about sex.

The passenger who requested the ride started it—before I even left my parking space.

"Tell the driver about the time you flashed the Uber driver in New Orleans!" he shouted.

He then told me that if I drove well, I'd get the same tip. (Spoiler alert: I did not get the same "tip." In fact, even though they paid the absurd nightly room charge at the Montage, they didn't tip at all.) The conversation went downhill from there.

The ride requester was a prototypical, overgrown frat boy. He was clearly overserved and acted like a grade-A douchenozzle the entire ride. In fact, he was such a clown that the last fifteen minutes of the ride were the most awkward and uncomfortable I've ever experienced.

As I drove, he recounted he and his wife's upside-down pineapple life. He then attempted to persuade the other couple to join them in the chaos.

FRIENDS LIKE THESE

On another awkward ride, one of Kat's friends (featured in a previous chapter) spent the whole ride home giving her friend graphic details about what would happen in her bedroom when she returned home to her man. Based on her level of intoxication, I doubt her boyfriend got her to the bedroom before she passed out.

I know I've picked up strippers. One stripper even offered a lap dance as a tip when I drove her to work after she got a DUI. I'm also reasonably sure I drove prostitutes on their way to or from work. Speaking of prostitutes . . .

I thought I was picking up a couple in Savannah. I don't know Savannah very well, so I didn't recognize the addresses. I pulled up at the pick-up location—a police substation—and started looking for Katie.

Katie and her friend were standing with a couple of police officers outside of the cops' cruisers. If I read their outfits correctly, assuming they were prostitutes seemed logical. They wore short, tight, sparkly dresses, and every inch of their outfits, hair, and makeup were decidedly disheveled.

Steeling myself for another awkward ride, I asked the two how they were doing as they climbed into my car.

"Been better," they answered in unison.

Then they launched into a conversation that allowed me to glean what happened. Turns out it wasn't a police station. And they weren't prostitutes. It was a medical clinic, and they were just basic white girls.

Katie went so hard celebrating her birthday that she required medical attention. Actually, that's not quite right. Katie and all her friends went so hard that their memories and decision-making skills degraded. Somehow, they made it back to their apartment, but Katie had passed out. Cold. So cold her friends had to drag her up the stairs.

The combination of intoxication and Katie's dead weight made the task difficult. One friend fell and got hurt attempting to drag Katie up the stairs. After a heroic effort, Katie's friends gave up, left Katie on the steps, and went to bed. Thankfully, a neighbor saw Katie and called EMS.

When Katie's dear friends awoke, they realized their friend—a drunk twenty-something whom they left half-dressed outside on the steps—was gone. Fortunately, they eventually found out where she was, and headed to the hospital to get her.

During the car ride home, they tried to convince Katie that they'd been drugged by someone at the bar. But after listening to their pride in taking shot after shot, it sounded like they just got hammered.

With friends like these, I really hope Katie doesn't have enemies.

CUP O' MORNING REGRET

I've provided many regret-filled morning rides and awkward rides of shame.

I once picked up someone I knew from a house that wasn't hers. It was Saturday morning, and she had on the same clothes she was wearing the night before when I dropped her off downtown.

When she came out of the door and saw me, horror flashed across her face. The ride home was spent in utter silence. I have no idea whose house she stayed at that night, but I got a one-star rating that morning and never got another ride request from her.

Another late-night ride was less awkward but equally revealing. It was a late-night pickup from the Fillin' Station, a local dive bar. 1 picked up a couple and took them to a beautiful home in a nearby neighborhood. They got very cozy in the backseat. Laughter and joking were interspersed with short moments of silence. Nothing unusual there, except this is a small town. And while he was too drunk to recognize me, I was sober. I knew the woman he was with wasn't his wife. And I wasn't taking them to the same house where I previously dropped off the passenger and his wife.

#UberProTip—Choose your friends wisely, and don't leave your friend passed out on the steps to your apartment.

YOU'VE GOTTA BE FREAKING KIDDING ME

"Truth is stranger than fiction, but it is because fiction is obliged to stick to the possibilities; truth isn't."—Mark Twain

This chapter contains the stories that don't fit anywhere else. Each of these stories still make me stop and shake my head in disbelief.

As you know, I stopped accepting rides with stops. I did this because I didn't want to facilitate drug transactions any longer, but that's not the only reason. Rides with stops suck. The wait time fee isn't worth the time it adds to the ride. Besides, most rides with stops are short, minimum-fare rides, and I make no money on the return trip. These are often booked by people who don't want to make the five-minute walk to a gas station or liquor store.

THREE DOORS OPEN

While this story doesn't involve a violent crime, it's almost that bad. It was one of those short, gas station roundtrips, the type of ride that generally doesn't result in tips. So, before the passenger buckled up, I knew the ride was a waste of my time. Honestly, I don't know why I accepted it. Maybe I was trying to hit a bonus or something. I don't remember. But I wasn't thrilled about taking the ride.

To make matters worse, at the pickup point, no one came out. When I messaged the passenger, she told me the ride wasn't for her. It was for her boyfriend. Now the ride really sucked. It was a minimum-fare drive for someone who didn't order the ride, and I was stuck making eleven cents a minute while I waited for the boyfriend to show his face.

Per Uber policy, I had to wait seven minutes before I could cancel the ride and earn a cancellation fee. After about six minutes and thirty seconds, dude and three of his friends roll out of the apartment and saunter toward the car. They get in, and we start the short, financially unrewarding trip to the gas station.

Remember when I explained that some rides came with a weed odor so strong I had to roll down the windows to avoid a contact high? This was one of those rides. It was bad. It only got worse at the gas station.

Before I could park, the dude in the front seat threw open his door.

"That's the m-f'er right there!" he shouted.

His boys followed his lead. I screeched to a stop. All three doors were wide open, and they jumped out of the car yelling at their mortal enemy who stood by a sign advertising discount cigarettes.

Words were exchanged, and then it was on. Fists started

flying, and we had a full-scale brawl popping off in the Circle K parking lot.

I had no intention of sticking around to see what happened next, but all three of my car doors dangled open with no one to close them. Unwilling to get out of the car, I took my chances. I threw the car in reverse and sped out of there, thanking God no one was in my way and that no one in the parking lot showed a gun.

SWINGERS ON THE SOUTH END

On to the next one.

I was on Hilton Head Island. It was late Saturday night, and rates surged at three times the normal rate, making every ride a good one. At this point, I was looking for a ride headed toward home that would allow me to make money as I drove home. My phone pinged with a ride request that would take me back to Centerfolds, Hilton Head's only strip club.

As I rolled up, my mood soured. Just outside the front door was some guy who could barely stand up. I crossed my fingers that he wasn't my ride and pulled up to the building. I didn't want to end my night worrying that my final passenger would vomit all over my car.

I stopped at the entrance and asked for Scott. One of the guys outside pointed toward the drunk guy who was barely on his feet. The less drunk guy tried to put Scott in my car, but it was useless. Scott couldn't function enough to help with this simple task.

At that point, I bit the bullet. I explained that I wasn't taking Scott anywhere unless someone came with him. I expected this would get me out of the ride, but I was wrong.

The guy who was trying to shove Scott in the car agreed.

"Okay, I'll go with him," the friend said, "but I need you to wait for me. I've got to go back into the club and get my wife."

Yes, you read that correctly. Drunken Scott's good pal needed me to wait while he went back into the club to retrieve his wife.

"Sure," I said, wondering if I was on the wrong planet or part of a prank show. "The more the merrier."

A couple minutes later, drunk Scott's friend returned, wife in tow. With one glance, I knew she wasn't just his wife. She was his clearly pregnant wife! Yes, dude and his great-with-child wife were taking staggeringly drunk Scott home.

They entered the vehicle, and the four of us took off. As we proceeded toward Bluffton, I learned yet another intriguing fact. Scott's guardian angels didn't even know Scott. The guy who ordered the ride was just being a good Samaritan by paying for an Uber at surge rates that were three times the normal fare.

Despite this, Scott wasn't cooperative. He couldn't even get the synapses to spark enough to give us his address. .

Instead, he just kept mumbling, "Gated community . . . just over bridge . . ."

We were getting nowhere fast, and the good Samaritan had exhausted his supply of patience. We stopped at a gas station and pulled out Scott's wallet to check his ID for an address. That was a bust. Dude wasn't local. He was from Atlanta, and I wasn't taking him that far.

I didn't know what to do, but the good Samaritan did. Having lost all patience with Scott, the Samaritan flagged down another Uber driver at the gas pump. He offered $20 for the other driver to take Scott to his undetermined destination.

For some unfathomable reason, the driver accepted the money. Before the guy could change his mind, we transferred incoherent Scott and bolted. Remember, this whole ride occurred at a hefty surge rate, and we were at least twenty minutes and ten miles into the ride.

Thrilled to get rid of drunk dude, I asked good Samaritan where I should take him. He gave me the address to an oceanfront home back on the south end of Hilton Head. I knew the ride would make my night much longer, as it would put me more than an hour from home. But, it also doubled how much I made on the ride.

As the trip began, the conversation focused on our joy at getting rid of drunk Scott. I relaxed, thinking the weird was all wrung out of this trip. Then the conversation took a hard left turn.

Apparently, this couple used to be swingers. Once they started having kids, they gave up swinging. However, they still enjoyed hitting the strip club together. They also joined some weird religious cult, and they spent the remainder of the trip telling me about it.

Once we arrived at their oceanfront home, my head was spinning, trying to process the ride's events and calculate how much I made with the swinger-turned-cult-member couple in tow. As the man exited the vehicle, he walked around to my window, pulled out a wad of cash, and handed me a $100 bill. Guess he didn't spend all his money at the club.

By this point, it was after 2 a.m. I started the hour-long

trip home and turned off the app. I wasn't about to find out what other tricks the night had up its sleeve.

> **#UberProTip**—Expect the unexpected. Even when you do, you'll be surprised. Also, $100 tips put you in the hall of fame, no matter how weird the ride was.

ZERO FS GIVEN

"Are you insane?" he asked. "Yes," she answered without a pause.

My biggest takeaway from my time as an Uber driver is a true appreciation for what those in the service industry deal with every day. Growing up, playing and coaching sports took up all my time. As a result, I never worked in a service industry job. However, I was raised to treat everyone with respect.

I also learned not to look down on someone who was working for a living. I've always been a good tipper because my favorite high school coach taught me by example that a big tip is a big deal. It also seemed like the right thing to treat people well when they were taking care of you.

In short, we should treat people the way we would want to be treated. Rideshare driving gave me ample opportunity to realize that many people don't abide by that simple principle.

I'd seen people get treated poorly in public. But nothing prepared me for how alcohol and anonymity could magnify arrogance and entitlement. Of course, some people don't need alcohol or anonymity to act like jerks. Many people truly believe Uber drivers are beneath them. These folks assume drivers are unskilled, unintelligent, and willing to serve as a personal valet as long as they need you—all for the low price of $20.

Fortunately, I dealt with angry people before rideshare driving. As a coach, every cut player and every substitution angered another parent. This gave me plenty of practice making the best decision possible and dealing with the people who disagree. Considering my professional career, you could say I've had decades of experience of dealing with angry people. However, I've never been verbally attacked as often or with the same level of venom as has occurred over the course of my 10,000 rideshare rides.

Perhaps the app is the problem. I suspect technology causes many to forget that the driver is a human, not an autonomous bot that can be beckoned with a smartphone. Add alcohol to technological disconnection, and you end up with a lot of passengers who lose their mind when they don't get their way.

This chapter details the most extraordinary jerks I've driven, but first some conversations that leave me shaking my head.

TALKING HEADS

Woman to her husband: "Don't talk to him like that."

Man to wife: "He's a f*****g Uber! I'll talk to him however I want."

Passenger one: "Did you tip him, bro?"

Passenger two: "Bro, he's a f*****g Uber. You don't tip those motherf*****s!"

Passenger one: "Hurry up, you've already made the driver wait."

Passenger two: "F*** him, he's f*****g Uber. Who cares?"

Then there's the conversation with an angry drunk bro. Beaufort's Water Festival is in full force, but the guy keeps giving me wrong pickup address.

Me: "Looks like this address is wrong, too. I'm just going to cancel the ride."

Him: "Come pick me up, motherf*****. I'll tip you $50. That's more f*****g money than your stupid f*****g a$$ will make all night."

Me: "Me I'd love to make an extra $50 on this ride, but I'm not sure picking you up is worth it. And since you can't even tell me where you are, I'm not sure how I'm going to pick you up."

Him: "F*** you, you stupid motherf*****. I don't want your stupid f*****g a$$ picking me up anyway, motherf*****."

With those conversations as an appetizer, let me introduce you to the three worst passengers I've ever met.

FLANNERY—FRIDAY NIGHT FREAK OUT

It was a typical Friday night in a small town. Rides took me all over town, but nothing memorable had occurred. My next pickup was in an upscale neighborhood on the waterfront. When I arrived, no one was there. I messaged the passenger and waited a couple of minutes. Then called but got no response.

I figured it would be a short ride, and canceling would probably net me just as much as taking the ride. But I didn't want to leave anybody hanging. So, being the nice guy, I called again when the timer hit zero. Someone answered.

She was angry that I wasn't in the right place, even though I was exactly where she sent me. I tried to explain, but she didn't want to hear it. When she paused, I spoke up. I asked her to tell me where she was, so I would come get her. She complained some more but told me. I headed her way.

This often happens late at night. People's drunk hands move their pins away from their actual location, and they don't check whether they send the driver to the right location.

Soon, I made it to my ride's location and pull into the driveway. Since we just talked on the phone, it should be a smooth process. Especially since I could have canceled and gotten paid. The lady on the phone had my name, the make and model of my car, my picture, and my license plate number. The only identifying information I had was her name.

Fortunately, the lady was waiting in the driveway. As soon as I pulled up, I recognized her. She was a prominent professional in the community. This wasn't uncommon. Remember—I took most of my rides in a small town, so if I spent all night in town, I would likely run into at least one passenger I knew, even if it wasn't a certainty that they would recognize me.

Before I could get my window rolled down, the F bombs started flying. Boiled down, her message was something like, "We've been waiting so long. Where have you been?"

I tried to diffuse the situation and ensured her I was here

to take her home. Unfortunately for me, her fuse had already been lit, and there was no turning back. Rather, she changed her tactics. Something inside her drunken professional brain decided I was going to kidnap her. In an instant, she switched from yelling about me being late to suspicion.

"What's my f*****g name motherf****r?" she screamed. And she didn't say it once. She said it over and over, like the chorus for a new hip-hop song.

As she screamed, her chance at entering my car dwindled to zero. Despite this, I couldn't help but try to reason with her. After all, I didn't want this drunken lady spreading tales about the Uber driver who tried to kidnap her.

I gave my name and explained again that I was there to pick her up. I encouraged her to verify this by checking her app. There, she could see my picture and verify that I'm driving the same vehicle with the same license plate number I was supposed to be driving.

Unfortunately, my calm reasoning didn't get past the liquor blocking her ears. Instead, this thirty-something lady screamed all the louder.

"What's my f*****g name, motherf****r?"

Convinced she was a lost cause, I cut my losses, canceled the ride on the app, and started to drive away. Realizing she wasn't going to get wherever she wanted to go, she changed tactics once again.

"Where are you f*****g going, you motherf****r?" she screamed.

Since my other comments didn't register, I ignored her question. This didn't please her. It was obvious, because she chased after me and launched one of her heels at my car.

Only Uber drivers get cussed up and down and have well-respected, prominent members of the community chase them down a driveway and drunkenly throw shoes at them.

FRANK—YO QUIERO TACO BELL!

A frequent point of contention between my passengers and I involves late-night drive-through requests. From a business perspective, creeping through a drive-through line makes no sense. It doubles the ride time without any increase in earnings. On top of that, it often costs my next ride. Soon as my waiting riders see me stop moving on the app, they cancel.

That said, I'm open to most requests if the passenger will fairly compensate me for my time. When I tell passengers that, their hunger typically subsides. Occasionally we make a mutually beneficial financial arrangement, and we proceed to the drive-through. These people understand capitalism.

Because I drive in a military town, I drive a lot of Marines around. To date, I've never had a problem with a group of Marines. They may get kind of rowdy as a group, but there's always one who makes sure no one gets in any trouble. A car full of Marines is an easy ride. (Except: The one who vomited all over my car.)

The only time any Marines gave me trouble was when one would get in the car with his girlfriend. They tended to be more problematic, but usually nothing of consequence happened.

Frank proved that there is an exception to every rule.

It was a Saturday night. I rolled up to Luther's to pick up Frank and his wife. From the smell that followed them into the car, they had enjoyed a large amount of beer. Before getting off Bay Street, Frank demanded a Taco Bell detour. The night was popping, and surge price was in effect. Frank's idea was a no-go.

I gave him my standard pitch to explain why I didn't do stops and hoped Frank was good at math. Unfortunately, he wasn't. He offered me $5 to do it. I again declined and explained that surge pricing made any other ride worth more than $5. He couldn't wrap his drunk mind around this and demanded I do his bidding. I repeated that $5 wasn't worth it and I would happily take them home or back to Luther's, but Taco Bell was out of the question.

This was more than Frank could take. He demanded that I stop the car and let them out. He felt I had disrespected him, and he wouldn't stay in my car another moment. I was more than happy to accommodate his request. Frank's ride was a long one. It would have taken me forever to get back downtown to take advantage of the surge pricing. In all sincerity, Frank did me a solid.

Fast forward to the end of the night.

I took three more rides during the next hour, each one was an easy ride at surge prices. Meanwhile, Frank the hothead struggled to find a new ride. As I passed Bay and Bladen, Frank and his wife were still standing where he demanded I let him out.

Here's hoping he got back to base eventually, without another ounce of disrespect.

FLETCHER—A LOVER OR A FIGHTER?

Have you ever challenged your Uber driver to a fight?

Fletcher did.

Fletcher is the type of passenger I never want in my car. After picking him up just once, there is zero chance I would ever let him into my car again, but—as they say—live and learn.

Marina pickups are always a gamble. There are a lot of variables in play when picking someone up at a marina. There could be a single sailor who needs a quick ride to a grocery store or hardware store for supplies. Or there could be a carload of frat boys who are hammered when they step off the boat at 1 p.m.

Fletcher is the reason I often don't take the marina gamble. Dressed like a cast member from Southern Charm, Fletcher was waiting for me with his girlfriend and their friends when I arrived in my Honda Civic. As expected, they got pissed that I could only fit four passengers. And if they wanted to bring their coolers and bags, they were out of luck. They should have ordered a bigger vehicle.

When Fletcher realized his Yeti was too big to fit in my trunk with his group's other bags, he passive-aggressively cursed me under his breath. To appease precious Fletcher, I compromised. I told him since the ride was so short, he could put the cooler in the backseat, and he could ride up front.

He accepted the solution, but he still wasn't happy. While we situated his girlfriend and cooler in the backseat, he continued complaining. As I waited to pull out of the parking lot, I got his attention.

"It's time to chill," I said. "Otherwise, you can find another ride."

This did not please Fletcher. He launched into a tirade as we pulled onto Sea Island Parkway. All the while, his girlfriend was apologizing for his behavior from the backseat. Her embarrassed apologies soon shifted to anger as Fletcher continued to behave like a petulant toddler.

At the start of Fletcher's tirade, his girlfriend was visibly mortified. She tried to shut him up, but that only enraged him more. When he threatened to whip my tail, I told him the ride was over and pulled up to a dive bar. During this short ride I watched his girlfriend's embarrassment turn to anger, but this was the final straw. His girlfriend lost her mind—fortunately not at me. The once-apologetic young lady ripped Fletcher a new one as she exited the car with her bag. He followed after her, dragging his Yeti from the backseat.

Before I zoomed away, he again promised to whip my tail—after he dealt with his girl. As a final display of power, Fletcher left the door open as he lumbered after his girlfriend who was stomping back in the direction of the marina.

#UberProTip—Just because you don't know your driver doesn't mean he doesn't know you. Oh, and getting home is more important than getting Taco Bell.

#BonusUberProTip—Don't threaten your driver or you'll get left on the side of the road with a super mad girlfriend.

EPILOGUE

After a few years of driving for Uber and Lyft, I figured out the best ways to make rideshare driving work. But I couldn't stop paying attention or learning. Otherwise, the ever-working, ever-changing algorithm would beat me at the game. Honestly, part of the thrill of driving was the cat-and-mouse game I played with the algorithm. I constantly worked to ensure I used the rideshare companies to make money and not get exploited by them.

Uber wanted me to accept every ride and never cancel any, but that only benefited them, not me. The more selective I was in taking rides, the better it worked for me. But making it work consistently wasn't easy. I never had enough information, so I always depended on the luck of the draw to get rides worth taking.

Then the pandemic came. That little virus upended the world and reworked the rideshare calculus. Driving strangers around suddenly seemed like a bad idea. I contemplated ways to create more effective income streams and began working on several of them.

By the time passengers felt comfortable using the apps again, I'd almost hung up my rideshare keys. Too many rides just weren't worth taking. That's when the companies rolled out upfront pricing to drivers in my market. This reduced the house's advantage. Now I had the information to determine whether a ride was worth taking or not.

In this new world, driving in small towns and small markets could work to my advantage because of the limited number of drivers. The town's small size also helped, making it easier to identify rider patterns, which helped me become a more efficient driver. My acceptance rate plunged to less than twenty percent.

Even though I declined eight out of ten requests, my weekly and monthly pay increased, because I was only taking profitable rides. In addition, seeing what requests I declined gave me more data that increased my understanding of tactics used to manipulate drivers into taking rides.

By only taking rides that were worth taking, I made the same amount of money in less time. I converted some of my extra time into writing this book.

Because I was driving in such a small market, I watched as Uber adjusted fares when I didn't accept a ride. I noticed the same ride pop up over and over and marveled as the fare rose each time. It became a game. I declined many rides until they became worth taking.

Now, the algorithm has gotten trickier. Sometimes it offers me a ride I previously declined for even less money. I'm not sure how the powers that be thought that would work.

As I learned the system, I was almost a true, independent contractor. In a roundabout way, I set my own rates. But the good times were short-lived. It wasn't long before soldiers disembarked from the Trojan horse of upfront pricing.

The rideshare companies' Odysseus came in the form of a massive rate cut. Of course, it wasn't presented as a rate cut.

It was packaged as a rate increase, but as I explained in the chapter on upfront pricing, only a very small, specific type of ride was of benefit to drivers. Rideshare execs recognized that while inflation may be bad for the general public, it worked to their benefit. Rising prices meant more people needed extra income. This increased the numbers of new drivers who were desperate to offset rising prices from inflation. These new, desperate drivers are ideal drivers, as they will accept any and all rides offered.

I've made a fair amount of money driving for rideshare companies. However, it's hard to nail down my actual profit, since the expenses are constant. Since my first ride, I've driven nearly 250,000 miles with paid passengers laughing, singing, screaming, and puking. Whatever my profit has been, the rideshare companies have made even more from my labor.

The real value of my driving experience is what I learned about people and human nature. Every mile has provided a master's-level practicum in business, sociology, and psychology. The knowledge and perspective I've gained by driving strangers is invaluable. Thanks to subtle and not-so-subtle clues passengers provide, I know how a ride will go before the passenger gets in the car.

This education hasn't answered all my questions though. Some questions seem beyond comprehension, such as:

What makes one customer pay $40 when asked for $20, while another tries to pay $25 for a $40 ride?

What makes one customer polite and kind—engaging in conversation about my life and family—while others see drivers as hired help undeserving of common courtesy or dignity?

FIVE STAR RIDES

What makes one customer thank me for doing my job, while another curses me while going out of my way to help them?

The answers aren't found in a person's ethnicity, gender, or socio-economic status. I've had the same experiences with minimum-wage workers ending their restaurant shifts and millionaires arriving on private planes. There's something deeper going on.

My driving experience reiterated how important both ends of a service transaction are. The business or individual providing the service is obliged to provide excellent service that corresponds with the amount charged for the service. While you can charge whatever you decide is a fair price and the market will bear, exploiting and manipulating customers and contractors is not a healthy business model.

On the other side of the transaction coin, customers are obliged to treat the person serving them with respect and dignity, regardless of how much (or how little) they charge. The customer also must align expectations with the price of services. In other words, don't expect fine dining levels of service at fast-food prices.

These experiences have sparked a desire to become an entrepreneur and control who profits off my time and energy. After decades of being tethered to a daily and yearly schedule, the freedom to set my own schedule has been refreshing. In the same way, tying my income to how hard I work and how well I do my job opens a realm of possibility I never experienced while working for a set salary schedule determined by experience instead of merit. Because of rideshare driving, I'll never think the same way. Careers in which someone tells me when to work and pays me the same amount regardless of the quality of work have lost their luster. I'm inspired to pass these ideas to my children, as the value of this type of freedom can't be measured only in dollars and cents.

Driving also opened my eyes to the myriad ways big companies like Lyft, Uber, Amazon, Google, and Facebook manipulate people to increase the company's market share and profit margins. You can't be truly free if you use products that rely on psychology to modify your behaviors in ways that benefit the company and are detrimental to individual users and society.

I've also spent a lot of time considering how a company's treatment of employees directly affects the customer service those employees provide. Service workers should expect to be treated with dignity by their employers and those they serve. Customers, likewise, should get treated fairly and served respectfully and competently by the company and their employees. When any of these relationships falls out of alignment, the whole process breaks down. If a company doesn't value its employees, they're unlikely to provide customers with the type of experience the company wants customers to have. In the same way, customers are less likely to give employees the dignity and kindness they deserve if the employees don't serve in a competent, professional manner or if they're being exploited by the company's business model.

I see the results of this misalignment every time I turn on the rideshare company's apps. Customers are solely motivated by getting where they need to go as quickly and inexpensively as possible. Most consumers aren't concerned about how their inexpensive ride impacts anyone else. The companies are motivated solely to make as much money on as many rides as possible. Companies aren't concerned about driver well-being unless it impacts driver availability. Drivers are caught in the middle, as the only way to meet customer and company goals is to work as much as possible for the least possible pay.

Most of all, driving has caused me to reflect on what freedom really is and the implications of how people treat each other. Transitioning to a life of earning my income as an independent contractor and entrepreneur has afforded me a great deal of freedom.

Over the past several years, I've been able to do things that I couldn't do with a traditional job. I've gone places I couldn't have gone when my schedule was set by an employer. Of course, this has drawbacks, too. The transactional nature of this type of commerce isn't nearly as fulfilling as working as a teacher and coach.

None of this would have been possible without the decision to give rideshare driving a try many years ago. It started out a strictly financial decision. But that decision turned out to be an unexpected catalyst for dramatic change. Even though rideshare driving is difficult and would never work for me full time, it served as my entry into a world where I controlled my schedule, a world where my income is determined by my effort and ability instead of being capped by education and experience. It opened my eyes to the possibility of designing a life that makes sense for my family and allows me to do those things I think are important. Driving got me out of the rat race.

On the other hand, freedom isn't reduced to doing whatever I want whenever I want to do it. Not considering how my actions impact others is a dangerous way to behave. That type of boundless, selfish freedom is destructive. It's unhealthy for individuals and societies.

As these crazy rideshare stories bounce around in your head, think about why you're doing what you're doing. Don't let big tech companies manipulate you into acting against your own self-interest to pad their profits. And always, always—ALWAYS—tip your Uber driver.